A LICENSE FOR BIAS
Sex Discrimination,
Schools, and Title IX

AAUW Legal Advocacy Fund

Published by the American Association of University Women Legal Advocacy Fund
1111 Sixteenth St. N.W.
Washington, DC 20036
202/785-7750
Fax: 202/ 785-8754
TDD: 202/ 785-7777
laf@aauw.org
www.aauw.org

Printed in the United States
First printing: November 2000
Cover design: Sabrina Meyers
Layout: John Sauerhoff
Editor: Susan Morse

Library of Congress Card Number: 00-192404
ISBN 1-879922-26-6

Printed on
recycled paper

019-01
11-00/5m

Table of Contents

Preface

In fulfilling its mission of supporting women fighting sex discrimination in higher education, the American Association of University Women Legal Advocacy Fund sees many cases brought under Title IX, the federal law prohibiting sex discrimination in institutions of education that receive federal funds. Unfortunately, while Title IX has great potential to create gender-fair schools, public misperceptions about the law's scope plague its implementation, and recent legislative and legal developments threaten enforcement efforts.

The public misperception that Title IX applies only to sports is understandable. Since the law's passage in 1972, women and girls have seen tremendous gains in athletic opportunities and resources. These successes have captured the American psyche, as evidenced by the nation's enthusiastic response to the 1999 U.S. victory in the Women's World Cup soccer tournament.

However, these playing field triumphs tend to overshadow Title IX's much broader mandate to eliminate sex discrimination in all areas of publicly funded education. Title IX is the shoehorn meant to guarantee girls and women access to higher education and career education, better employment opportunities, increased opportunities in mathematics and science, protection against sexual harassment, standardized testing that is free of gender bias, and fair treatment of pregnant and parenting students.

The focus on women's sports also feeds a wide misperception that we, as a nation, have achieved the goal of Title IX and that our educational institutions are gender-fair. Far from it.

To dispel the popular belief that Title IX is a sports equity law and to determine the effectiveness of the legislation, the AAUW Legal Advocacy Fund embarked upon a research project to analyze the enforcement of Title IX in non-sports-related cases.

This research analyzes non-sports-related Title IX complaints filed with the Department of Education's Office for Civil Rights (OCR)—the primary Title IX enforcement agency—from 1993 through 1997. It examines the kinds of complaints filed (sexual harassment, discipline, admissions, etc.), the status of those making the complaints (students, teachers, males, females, etc.), and the actions taken in response by OCR.

Seventy percent of the Title IX complaints filed in the four-year period we examined were non-sports-related. And although the AAUW Legal Advocacy Fund recognizes and applauds OCR's progress toward enforcing Title IX, the report shows that more can be done. *A License for Bias* highlights continuing problems that impede enforcement efforts. These problems include over-tolerance for institutional foot-dragging, investigation procedures and complaint resolutions that vary widely from region to region, and inconsistency in initiating compliance reviews and monitoring compliance agreements.

A License for Bias outlines the obstacles to Title IX enforcement efforts and offers action agendas for Congress, the Office for Civil Rights, and educational institutions that will accelerate the equity advancements made possible by Title IX and ensure equitable educational institutions as we approach the 30th anniversary of this important legislation.

Patricia J. McCabe
Director, AAUW Legal Advocacy Fund

Acknowledgments

The AAUW Legal Advocacy Fund would like to extend our deep gratitude to the following contributors:

The Women's Sports Foundation deserves credit for the concept for this report. In 1997-1998 the Women's Sports Foundation had just completed a report on sports-related Title IX complaints and enforcement and suggested that the AAUW Legal Advocacy Fund examine the other areas covered by Title IX.

Beth Hoffman, a New York member of AAUW and practicing attorney, began work on the report in 1997. When she returned to the full-time practice of law, she passed the torch to two summer interns.

In summer 1998, Paula Zimmerman, who had just completed her first year at George Washington University National Law Center, continued collecting the data and prepared introductory material.

Because of delays in receiving documentation from OCR, the project extended to a second summer in 1999. Jennifer Engle, a doctoral candidate at American University, analyzed volumes of documentation and drafted the initial report. A very special thank you to Jennifer for her dedication and persistence on this project.

Heartfelt thanks also go to:

- LAF staff members Amy Falk and Courtney Chappell for reviewing multiple drafts of the report.

- Nancy Zirkin and Lisa Levine in AAUW's Public Policy and Government Relations Department, AAUW Association Director Amy Swauger, and AAUW Educational Foundation Research Director Pamela Haag, for critiquing early drafts of the report.

- LAF Advisory Committee members for reviewing the report.

- Outside reviewers Verna Williams, vice president and director of educational opportunities at the National Women's Law Center, and Donna Euben, general counsel of the American Association of University Professors, for providing valuable input to this project.

- Susan Morse, Sabrina Meyers, John Sauerhoff, and Carol L. Burnett in AAUW's Publications Department for their roles in the editing and production of the report.

The AAUW Legal Advocacy Fund would like to extend its appreciation to The Ford Foundation for its generous support for this important project.

A Timeline of the Development and Interpretation of Title IX

1965	Presidential Executive Order 11246 prohibits federal contractors from discriminating in employment on the basis of race, color, religion, or national origin.
October 13, 1968	Executive Order 11246 is amended by Executive Order 11375 to include discrimination on the basis of sex.
March 9, 1970	Representative Martha Griffith (D-Michigan) gives the first speech in Congress concerning discrimination against women in education. Three weeks later, the first contract compliance investigation involving sex discrimination begins at Harvard University.
June and July 1970	Representative Edith Green (D-Oregon) drafts legislation prohibiting sex discrimination in education and holds the first congressional hearings on the education and employment of women.
1970 -1972	A bill outlawing sex discrimination in education works its way through Congress. Proposed legislation (the now-famous Title IX) includes an amendment to the Equal Pay Act—enforced by the Department of Labor—extending protection against sex discrimination to administrators, professionals, and executives.
June 8, 1972	Congress passes Title IX.
June 23, 1972	President Nixon signs Title IX into law.
July 1, 1972	Title IX takes effect.
1972-1975	The U.S. Department of Health, Education, and Welfare Office for Civil Rights develops regulations for Title IX.
May 27, 1975	President Ford signs the Title IX regulations.
July 1975	Title IX regulations take effect.
1975-1979	The HEW Office for Civil Rights develops policy interpretations on issues such as athletics.
1979	The Department of Education Organization Act is signed into law, turning HEW education offices into a separate Department of Education and renaming HEW the Department of Health and Human Services.

May 4, 1980	The Department of Education is established.
1984	The U.S. Supreme Court rules in *Grove City College v. Bell* that Title IX is program specific and that, therefore, only those programs and activities receiving direct federal funds need comply.
1988	Congress passes the Civil Rights Restoration Act, restoring Title IX liability to an entire school system or college if it receives federal education funds.
1992	The U.S. Supreme Court acknowledges in *Franklin v. Gwinnet County Public Schools et al.* that institutions can be held liable for acts of sex discrimination by individuals in those institutions. This landmark case also holds that plaintiffs can sue for monetary damages.
1998	The U.S. Supreme Court holds in *Gebser v. Lago Vista Independent School District* that schools are liable for sexual harassment of students by teachers only when a school official who has authority to institute corrective measures has actual notice of the teacher's misconduct and is deliberately indifferent to the misconduct.
1999	The U.S. Supreme Court in *Davis v. Monroe County Board of Education* expands enforcement of Title IX by clarifying that institutions must address student-to-student sexual harassment. However, the applicable liability standard is the narrow one set forth in *Gebser.*

Executive Summary

In 1972 the U.S. Congress declared war on sex discrimination in education, enacting Title IX of the Education Amendments. The intent of the law was clear: "No person in the United States shall, on the basis of sex, be excluded from participation in, be denied the benefits of or be subjected to discrimination under any education program or activity receiving financial assistance."

Intent is one thing, however, and adherence another. Throughout the law's history, its effectiveness has hinged primarily on enforcement efforts by the U.S. Department of Education's Office for Civil Rights (OCR). *A License for Bias: Sex Discrimination, Schools, and Title IX* examines the scope of OCR's Title IX enforcement between 1993 and 1997. In keeping with the law's broad mandate, the report focuses on complaints outside athletics. For while the public best knows Title IX for leveling the playing field in school sports, the law regulates activity in a much wider realm, including course offerings, standardized testing, sexual harassment, and access to higher education.

A License for Bias identifies important trends and issues in Title IX complaints filed with OCR and analyzes the effectiveness of the agency's Title IX enforcement efforts. While recognizing that Title IX has improved the educational climate for women and girls in many ways, our report shows that enforcement efforts vary widely by region and are often hampered by the absence of guidelines and over-tolerance of institutional foot-dragging. The report offers suggestions for further boosting enforcement and making Title IX a more effective tool to combat sex discrimination in educational institutions.

Trends and Issues in Title IX Complaints

The sample of 425 cases reviewed here represents more than 60 percent of non-sports-related Title IX cases resolved by OCR during the four-year investigation period.

OCR is the administrative agency charged with enforcing the federal civil rights laws that prohibit discrimination on the basis of race, color, national origin, sex, disability, and age in educational programs and activities that receive federal financial assistance. OCR carries out its responsibilities by resolving complaints filed by students, parents, and others. About 5,000 cases are filed each year, 10 percent of which are sex-based Title IX complaints; the remainder concern other forms of discrimination barred by distinct laws. OCR also initiates its own investigations by conducting compliance reviews. Compliance reviews typically target systemic problems that are particularly acute or national in scope.

Case resolution involves (1) evaluating the complaint to ensure that it concerns an alleged civil rights violation that is within OCR's authority and that has been timely filed, and (2) attempting to resolve the complaint through resolution between the parties, negotiated agreements, investigation, and enforcement. If OCR is unable to achieve voluntary compliance, it can initiate an enforcement action in one of two ways: OCR may either (1) initiate administrative proceedings to suspend, terminate, or refuse to grant or continue federal financial assistance to the recipient, or (2) refer the case to the Department of Justice for judicial proceedings to enforce any rights of the United States under any U.S. law.

Compliance reviews initiated by OCR investigate particular school practices that may deny equal access to students or employees on the basis of sex. These reviews maximize the impact of OCR's resources and balance the enforcement programs. Experience shows that carefully targeted compliance reviews often result in policy or program changes that affect large numbers of students—unlike the individualized resolution of specific complaints. If an institution found in violation of the law will not voluntarily comply, OCR can move to enforce the law through administrative or legal proceedings.

Case and Complainant Information

Students and employees, both male and female, at all levels of education are protected under the mandate of Title IX and can seek remedy from sex discrimination by filing a complaint with the Office for Civil Rights. Our data revealed, however, that female students account for the overwhelming majority of complaints filed.

- Complaints filed by females accounted for 71 percent of cases; complaints by males, 29 percent. The higher proportion of complaints filed by females is not surprising, since females have traditionally been the underrepresented sex.

- Complaints by or on behalf of students account for the overwhelming number of sex discrimination cases filed with OCR. Students filed 91 percent of sex discrimination cases; by contrast, employees filed only 9 percent. (OCR has only limited jurisdiction over employee cases.)

- Complaints in elementary and secondary schools represented 56 percent of sex discrimination cases; complaints in colleges and universities, 44 percent.

Types of Complaints

Title IX prohibits sex discrimination in all areas of education, including admissions and recruitment, educational programs and activities, course offerings, counseling, financial aid, employment assistance, facilities and housing, health and insurance benefits and services, scholarships, athletics, and discrimination by marital and parental status. During our investigation period, the five most common complaints of sex discrimination (excluding sports-related cases) occurred in these areas:

(1) sexual harassment

(2) admissions, financial aid, and testing

(3) discipline

(4) procedural requirements

(5) retaliation

[1] Trends and Issues in Title IX Complaints
KEY FINDINGS:

- Nearly two-thirds (63 percent) of Title IX cases involved sexual harassment complaints.

- More than half (54 percent) of sexual harassment cases involved staff-to-student sexual harassment.

- More than one-quarter (28 percent) of sexual harassment cases involved peer-to-peer sexual harassment.

- 70 percent of complaints in elementary and secondary schools and 59 percent of complaints in higher education involved sexual harassment.

- 90 percent of Title IX cases filed on behalf of K-12 female students involved sexual harassment, while only 39 percent of cases filed on behalf of K-12 male students involved sexual harassment.

- 70 percent of Title IX cases filed on behalf of female college students involved sexual harassment, while only 39 percent of cases filed on behalf of male college students involved sexual harassment.

IMPLICATIONS:

Our findings document the pervasive problem of sexual harassment at all levels of education and reflect the extent to which grievance procedures in schools and universities do not adequately address incidents of sexual harassment.

RECOMMENDATIONS:

The findings support the continuing need for schools and universities to develop grievance procedures, mandated by law under Title IX, to address the pervasive problem of sexual harassment. In many instances, problems occur because procedural guidelines are absent or not followed. Schools and universities also need to take a more active role in addressing sexual harassment by conducting surveys and providing appropriate training to administrators, teachers, and staff. We recommend that OCR provide technical assistance to help schools and universities develop and implement such procedures and programs.

In light of recent court decisions affecting school liability for sexual harassment (*Gebser v. Lago Vista Independent School District (1998)* and *Davis v. Monroe County Board of Education (1999)*), we also recommend that OCR revise sexual harassment guidelines to help students and their parents meet the actual notice requirements under Title IX. Congressional action may also be needed to restore the broad mandate of the legislation in the wake of these court rulings.

[2] Admissions, Financial Aid, and Testing

KEY FINDINGS:

- 43 percent of sex discrimination cases filed on behalf of college students involved complaints of unfair practices in admissions, financial aid, and testing. This category of complaints includes admissions, enrollment, retention, dismissal, testing, evaluation, and financial aid.

- 62 percent of these cases were filed on behalf of male students; 38 percent, on behalf of female students.

IMPLICATIONS:

The data reveal that both sexes perceive discrimination in admissions and testing. For male students, the majority of complaints allege that college and university admissions give preference to female students; however, OCR substantiated none of these complaints. In contrast, female student complaints regarding standardized testing were substantiated. In a much-publicized case, OCR found that the Educational Testing Service and the College Board discriminated against girls by using a gender-biased exam (the Preliminary Scholastic Assessment Test, or PSAT) as the sole basis for selecting National Merit Scholarship winners and as a factor in college admissions decisions.

RECOMMENDATIONS:

Based on the findings in this case, we recommend that OCR initiate several high-profile compliance reviews on sex discrimination in standardized testing. We also recommend that colleges and universities review their policies regarding the use of standardized tests that unfairly limit admissions and scholarship opportunities for women.

[3] Discipline

- 20 percent of Title IX cases at the elementary and secondary level involved complaints of unfair treatment in student discipline.

- Roughly two-thirds of discipline cases were filed on behalf of male students, often male students of color; the remaining one-third were filed on behalf of female students.

IMPLICATIONS:

Our findings indicate that lack of enforcement of Title IX hurts both girls and boys. Nearly 30 percent of the complainants in our four-year sample were male. Boys are particularly affected by or most often claim unfair discipline in schools, although the evidence in OCR investigations did not substantiate two-thirds of the discipline complaints by male students. Still the data reveal that sex discrimination affects both male and female students in schools.

RECOMMENDATIONS:

We recommend that OCR provide policy guidance to schools on student discipline. Schools need to understand their responsibilities for the fair treatment of all students, male and female. Given that statistics reveal at least the perception that male students are more harshly disciplined than female students, OCR should confront the problem by conducting compliance reviews, particularly with regard to male students of color.

[4] Procedural Requirements

KEY FINDINGS:

- More than a third (34 percent) of Title IX cases involved complaints about alleged school failures to follow federal mandates to develop grievance procedures, designate equity representatives, and post public notices of nondiscrimination.

- Most complaints alleging a failure to follow procedural requirements were filed in connection with sexual harassment complaints.

IMPLICATIONS:

The findings reveal that the federal mandate requiring every educational institution to establish grievance procedures for addressing sex discrimination, including sexual harassment, is widely ignored.

RECOMMENDATIONS:

In addition to establishing grievance procedures, schools and universities must appoint a representative to coordinate compliance activities as mandated by Title IX. Representatives help ensure that students and parents know their rights under Title IX. We recommend that OCR provide policy guidance on the activities that should be carried out by Title IX coordinators and that Congress appropriate funds to support these positions at the state and local level.

[5] Retaliation

KEY FINDINGS:

- Nearly a quarter (22 percent) of Title IX cases (and 64 percent of employee Title IX complaints) involved complaints of retaliation for engaging in a protected activity under Title IX, such as filing a sexual harassment complaint. Most retaliation complaints were filed on behalf of students and employees who said they were singled out for unfair treatment after filing sexual harassment complaints.

- Many schools and universities fail to institute federally mandated policies to protect students from retaliation for engaging in a protected activity under Title IX. Previous research has demonstrated that schools and universities without formal policies against sex discrimination are much less likely to take action against discrimination when it occurs.

As previously recommended, schools and universities must establish policies to protect students from all forms of sex discrimination, including retaliation for engaging in a protected activity. This is particularly important given that many students cite fear of retaliation as a reason not to report sex discrimination. (See sexual harassment case studies on page 37.)

Compliance Reviews

Out of the approximately 600 compliance reviews initiated during our four-year investigation, fewer than 20 dealt with sex discrimination. Even while sex discrimination complaints accounted for 10 percent of OCR's caseload, the agency devoted only 3.3 percent of its compliance reviews to this area of the law. During one year of our four-year investigation, regional offices initiated no compliance reviews involving sex discrimination. Five regional offices conducted no compliance reviews related to sex discrimination during our four-year investigation period. More than half of all sex discrimination compliance reviews were conducted by just two regional offices.

Recommendations

Based on our findings, we recommend that the Office for Civil Rights initiate substantially more compliance reviews related to sex discrimination issues. The agency should initiate such reviews at least in proportion to the number of sex discrimination complaints received by the agency. In 1997, 8 percent (431) of the 5,296 cases received by OCR related to sex discrimination, yet less than 2 percent (2) of the l52 compliance reviews initiated by the agency dealt with sex discrimination.[1]

OCR Investigation of Title IX Complaints

Filing of Complaints

The Office for Civil Rights regulates compliance with Title IX through the investigation and resolution of complaints filed with the agency. To initiate an investigation under Title IX, individuals must file a complaint with one of the 12 regional enforcement offices throughout the country within 180 days of the alleged discrimination. A complaint may be filed with OCR by anyone who believes that an institution covered by Title IX has discriminated against someone on the basis of sex.

To file a complaint with OCR, students and their parents must be aware of their rights under Title IX and must be prepared to exercise them.

- Notice of Title IX: Our findings reveal that many schools and universities have not established grievance procedures, and many more have not appointed a designated representative to address complaints of sex discrimination as mandated by law. As a result, students and employees may not know what acts constitute illegal sex discrimination under Title IX. Further, students and employees may not know they have the option to pursue an OCR action against an educational institution.

- Statute of Limitations Under Title IX: The problem is further compounded by the 180-day statute of limitations imposed by OCR on complaints of sex discrimination. Although OCR will grant extensions in some instances, not knowing about Title IX (or the agency) is not considered grounds for an extension.

Based on our investigation, we recommend that the Office for Civil Rights take the following actions to increase opportunities for students and employees to address sex discrimination in schools and universities:

- Create a complaint form with a checklist of possible areas of sex discrimination, and distribute copies of the form to elementary and secondary school principals and college and university presidents, provosts, and offices of academic affairs. School administrators can oversee the appropriate distribution of the form. This should help provide students and employees with greater knowledge of their rights under Title IX. The agency should continue to accept complaints submitted by letter with or without the complaint form.

- In every complaint of sex discrimination filed with the agency, investigate whether the institution has complied with the notice provisions, established grievance procedures, and designated an equity coordinator. Where institutions are found lax, include appropriate notice requirements in the compliance agreement and ensure future compliance through the monitoring process.

- Initiate more compliance reviews to determine whether institutions are meeting Title IX procedural requirements to appoint an equity coordinator and establish grievance procedures.

- Extend the OCR-imposed six-month statute of limitations for Title IX complaints to the two to three years allowed by the state and federal court system.

Investigation of Complaints

When a complaint is filed with the Office for Civil Rights, the agency enacts procedures to begin investigation of the incidents of sex discrimination alleged by the complainant.

- Acceptance of Title IX Complaints: Before the initiation of an investigation, OCR decides whether or not to accept the complaint of sex discrimination filed with the agency. During our period of investigation, OCR received more than 2,000 complaints, but assumed responsibility for fewer than 1,000. In other words, OCR declined to investigate more than half the complaints. Denials were most often based on jurisdiction and the statute of limitations.

- Undue Length of Investigation: Our research revealed an overly long investigative process. The average investigation took more than 200 days—nearly seven months. About 25 percent of the complaint investigations were not completed within 270 days (the length of a school year), and 10 percent still remained open after an entire calendar year. Several complaint investigations took nearly three years to complete (the longest took 959 days). Such delays are no small hardships for complainants who, before approaching OCR, have usually already endured the lengthy process of filing a complaint with the offending institution. In addition, when investigations take so long, the complainant may well have left the offending classroom and/or institution. Many potential complainants, therefore, may decide that filing a complaint is not worth their time if they will have distanced themselves from the problem by the time it is finally investigated. If they do complain, they will have to either put up with unbearable situations or put their education on hold.

- Length of Investigation by Region: Regional offices varied considerably in the average length of time they took to investigate complaints. Four regions completed investigations within six months, while the other eight regions completed investigations within about eight months.

- Investigation Procedures-Records and Data From Institution: During an investigation, OCR may attempt to collect information from an institution to make a determination in the case. However, some institutions do not maintain the records needed by OCR, thereby impeding the agency's investigation. In particular, many don't sort data by sex, making it hard for OCR to compare a complainant's situation with that of others of the opposite sex. Our research found that when comparison data is not made available to the agency by the institution, OCR cannot (and does not) make a determination of discrimination in the complaint investigation.

- Investigation Procedures-Records of Investigation by Institutions: The agency may also request the records of the educational institution's investigation into the complaint. OCR does not require an individual to file a complaint with the institution before seeking help from the agency. However, if the individual first appealed to the institution, OCR relies on information from that investigation in determining the merit of an OCR complaint. If the complainant does not attempt to use the institution's federally mandated grievance procedures (assuming it has them in place), it is unlikely the agency will find the institution in violation of allegations of sex discrimination. This practice is in conflict with the policies of the agency to investigate and resolve complaints on behalf of the complainant and independent of the institution.

- Investigation Procedures-Interviews: OCR does not maintain guidelines on the number of informants to be interviewed during an investigation or who these informants should be. Our research found that the agency sometimes relies more on interviews with faculty and administrators than on interviews with the complainant and other informants on behalf of the complainant. As a result, in these cases the agency's determination is more likely to reflect the perspective of the institution.

RECOMMENDATIONS:

Based on our investigation, we recommend the following actions to the Office for Civil Rights to improve the enforcement of Title IX through complaint investigation on behalf of students and employees in schools and universities:

- Establish measures (such as complaint forms) to outline the information needed from the complainant and to improve the rate at which complaints are accepted for investigation.

- Reduce investigation time to six months or less to more effectively address sex discrimination in schools and universities.

- Work with Congress to mandate that institutions collect employment, academic, and discipline records and sort the data by sex to facilitate the investigation of sex discrimination complaints.

- Establish measures to promote uniformity among regions on the investigation of complaints of sex discrimination. Each region should report on effective practices and procedures for improving complaint investigation.

- Designate specialists in sex equity and discrimination in each regional office and the national office to more effectively investigate complaints of sex discrimination.

Resolution and Monitoring of Complaints

The Office for Civil Rights may conclude an investigation by proceeding to complaint resolution. The agency can enter into negotiations with the institution at any time during the investigation or at the completion of the investigation to resolve the complaint. The negotiation of an agreement represents an effort by OCR to engage institutions in a voluntary resolution of the allegations in the complaint.

- Methods of Complaint Resolution: During our investigation period, 47 percent of complaints were resolved through the negotiation of an agreement with the institution. Coincidentally, in 47 percent of complaints, OCR found insufficient evidence to support a violation against the institution. No complaints were resolved through OCR's initiation of formal enforcement to deny federal funds to an institution.

- Disparities by Sex in Complaint Resolution: Our research found that more than half the complaints filed by females were resolved through a negotiated settlement. In contrast, 65 percent of complaints filed by males ended in dismissal for lack of sufficient evidence.

- Disparities by Regions in Complaint Resolution: Our investigation revealed that only four regions resolved complaints through the negotiation of a compliance agreement in more than 60 percent of cases. In two regions, roughly two-thirds of cases were dismissed following a determination of insufficient evidence. In another region, nearly 90 percent of cases were dismissed for the same reason.

- Complaint Resolution in Compliance Reviews: Our investigation found that compliance reviews were more effective for addressing sex discrimination than complaint resolution. Violations requiring corrective action were found in two-thirds of compliance reviews, compared with the finding of a violation in less than one-half of complaints filed with the agency. The period for monitoring the compliance agreement is also longer—five years—as compared to several months to two years for complaint resolution.

- Compliance Agreements: Our investigation found that OCR considers an institution to be in compliance with Title IX once it has accepted, but not necessarily implemented, terms of a post-investigation compliance agreement. In other words, institutions are routinely cleared even though violations remain. Designating an institution compliant before it has implemented the stipulated changes removes the impetus, or at least the immediate need, for the institution to remedy the problem of sex discrimination (although the institution will be monitored for compliance with the agreement).

- Regional Inconsistencies in Compliance Agreements: Our investigation found inconsistencies among the regional offices in the provisions of the compliance agreements. Regional offices often proposed disparate remedies to address similar problems of sex discrimination. There were also disparities between the offices in terms of the time allotted for monitoring compliance.

- Repeat Offenders: Our research revealed that a considerable number of institutions had multiple offenses during the investigation period. Nearly 15 percent of all cases involved institutions under investigation for multiple cases of sex discrimination. Most of these cases involved the same type of complaint. OCR sometimes allowed institutions with repeat violations to sign another compliance agreement addressing the same violations as previous agreements.

RECOMMENDATIONS:

Based on our investigation, we propose the following recommendations to improve the resolution and monitoring of Title IX complaints by the Office for Civil Rights:

- Establish measures to increase the proportion of complaints that proceed to negotiations and a compliance agreement.

- Designate institutions with outstanding violations as in conditional compliance until they have fully implemented the terms of the compliance agreement. Pursue harsher penalties for institutions that do not fully implement the agreements and for institutions with repeat violations of sex discrimination.

- Develop guidelines for regional offices to follow in taking action against institutions according to the type of violations addressed in the compliance agreement. Establish time frames for monitoring compliance agreements by regional offices.

- Increase the use of compliance reviews to more effectively address sex discrimination in educational institutions.

Action Agenda for Title IX

Agenda for Congress

- Increase federal funding to OCR to support the agency's mandate.

- Increase federal funding to support Title IX through the Women's Educational Equity Act and Title IV of the 1964 Civil Rights Act.

- Appropriate federal funding for OCR, the Office of Educational Research and other government agencies to pool collected data on sex discrimination in educational institutions in a national repository and develop national statistics.

- Distribute federal funding for educational institutions and state educational agencies to support sex equity coordinators.

Agenda for the Office for Civil Rights

- Address the issues in complaint investigation and resolution identified in our report and develop consistent procedures for the 12 regional offices to improve the handling of sex discrimination complaints.

- Extend the agency-imposed 180-day statute of limitations for Title IX.

- Develop a form with a checklist for filing complaints.

- Increase the proportion of sex discrimination complaints accepted for investigation by the agency.

- Complete investigations of complaints within six months.

- Develop guidelines for the negotiation of compliance agreements with institutions.

- Establish time frames for monitoring compliance agreements.

- Coordinate efforts between the national office and regional offices to implement reforms in complaint investigation and resolution by requiring each regional office to report on effective practices and procedures for addressing issues of sex discrimination.

- Designate equity specialists in sex discrimination issues in the national and regional offices.

- Increase the number of compliance reviews focused on sex discrimination issues in educational institutions.

- Develop guidelines to help educational institutions establish grievance procedures and appoint sex equity coordinators. Identify specific activities to be conducted by the sex equity coordinators.

- Revise sexual harassment guidelines in light of recent court decisions affecting the liability of educational institutions.

- Clarify regulations regarding discipline and standardized tests for admissions as forms of sex discrimination in institutions.

- Designate institutions with violations to be in conditional compliance during the implementation of the compliance agreement. Pursue harsher penalties for institutions that do not fully implement the agreements and for institutions with multiple offenses of sex discrimination.

- Work with Congress to mandate that schools and universities collect employment, academic, and disciplinary records and separate the information by sex to facilitate the investigation and resolution of sex discrimination complaints.

- Require institutions to submit compliance reports on a regular basis as a condition of receiving federal funds.

- Coordinate an interagency enforcement initiative to increase efforts to enforce Title IX in educational institutions. Each federal agency should develop plans for the enforcement of Title IX, including regulations and procedures for handling complaints of sex discrimination.

Agenda for Schools and Universities

- Adopt and publish grievance procedures on sex discrimination for students and employees, and develop and implement procedures for investigating and resolving sex discrimination complaints.

- Appoint and support an equity coordinator to monitor Title IX compliance.

- Collect employment, academic, and disciplinary records and separate the information by sex to facilitate the investigation and resolution of sex discrimination complaints by the institution and by outside agencies. Maintain records of investigations of sex discrimination complaints.

- Conduct annual compliance surveys to assess the problem of sex discrimination and submit compliance reports to the Office for Civil Rights on a regular basis as a condition of receiving federal funds.

- Conduct training for faculty, staff, and students to address the problem of sex discrimination in education. Allow faculty and staff to earn professional development credit for taking such courses. Provide faculty and staff with materials and resources to incorporate anti-bias content and pedagogy into the curriculum for students.

- Forge partnerships in the community with law enforcement agencies and community organizations. Establish partnerships with parents.

Introduction

No person in the United States shall, on the basis of sex, be excluded from participation in, be denied the benefits of, or be subjected to discrimination under any education program or activity receiving Federal financial assistance.

Title IX of the Education Amendments of 1972, 20 U.S.C. Section 1681

The Scope of Title IX

Title IX, the federal law prohibiting sex discrimination in education, was passed in 1972 to close the gaps in civil rights protections for women in education. In passing Title IX, Congress sought to provide women and girls increased access to educational opportunities at all levels of schooling. It also sought to offer protection to women employed by educational institutions.

Today, Title IX provides legal protection against sex discrimination for approximately 70 million students and employees in all educational institutions receiving federal financial assistance, including most public and private schools. Although many private elementary and secondary schools do not receive federal funds, most private post-secondary institutions do. Title IX also covers institutions such as vocational training centers, public libraries, and museums.

Institutions exempt from some or all provisions of Title IX include military schools, religious schools, and fraternities and sororities. A religious institution that is subject to Title IX may request an exemption from a particular legislative requirement if the institution can demonstrate that the requirement would be inconsistent with its religious tenets.[1]

Title IX legislation prohibits sex discrimination in all areas of education, including admissions and recruitment, educational programs and activities, course offerings, counseling, financial aid, employment assistance, facilities and housing, health and insurance benefits and services, scholarships, athletics, and discrimination based on marital and parental status.[2]

The Title IX regulations, established in 1975, stipulate specific practices and procedures required of all educational institutions subject to the law. Under these regulations, each institution has a responsibility to

- designate a Title IX coordinator to oversee compliance efforts and to investigate any complaints of sex discrimination,
- notify all students and employees of the activities of the Title IX coordinator, and
- publicize its grievance procedures and nondiscrimination policies on sex discrimination.

The regulations also required each educational institution to perform an evaluation of policies and procedures by July 1976 to determine its compliance with Title IX. Institutions that uncovered violations were required to develop plans for prompt remedial actions. A report of the evaluation and the corrective action plans were to have been kept on record for three years after completion.[3]

Unfortunately, this attempt by Congress to bring educational institutions into quick conformance with the law was widely ignored. Most institutions never conducted an initial evaluation for Title IX compliance. In any case, the persistence of sex discrimination in education over the last 30 years suggests the need for ongoing institutional evaluations of their compliance status.

The Impact of Title IX

In the nearly 30 years since the adoption of Title IX, there have been significant improvements for women and girls in education. To appreciate the progress, one need only review the conditions before Title IX:

- Many schools and universities had separate entrances for male and female students.

- Most medical and law schools limited the number of women admitted to 15 or fewer per school.

- Many colleges and universities required women to have higher test scores and better grades than male applicants to gain admission.

- Women students living on campus were not allowed to stay out past midnight, and women faculty members were excluded from the faculty club. They were encouraged to join the faculty wives' club instead.

- Married women were not allowed to attend some colleges and universities.

- Female students were not allowed to take certain courses, from physics to industrial arts.

- Pregnant students were often expelled from school and not welcomed back after they gave birth.[4]

Title IX has helped break down such barriers to equal opportunity and improve opportunities for women and girls at all levels of education. Here are just a few indicators:

- Since 1972, the percentage of bachelor's degrees awarded to women has increased from 38 percent to more than 56 percent today. Women are now awarded more than half of all master's degrees as well.[5]

- In 1972 women received only 9 percent of medical degrees, 1 percent of dental degrees, and 7 percent of law degrees. In 1994 women received 38 percent of medical degrees, 38 percent of dental degrees, and 43 percent of law degrees.

- Women make up more than 58 percent of students in postsecondary vocational education.

- The dropout rates for pregnant students have declined 30 percent between 1980 and 1990.[6]

While much has been accomplished since the enactment of Title IX, much remains to be done. Women and girls continue to face sex discrimination in many areas in education, including vocational education, higher education, standardized testing, and employment. Consider these facts:

- Although women earn more than half of bachelor's and master's degrees, they still earn just 39 percent of doctoral degrees.[7]

- Women continue to be significantly underrepresented as recipients of undergraduate and graduate degrees in mathematics, science, and engineering. At the doctoral level, women earn only 17 percent of degrees in mathematics, 14 percent of degrees in computer science, and 7 percent of degrees in engineering.[8]

- Women continue to score lower than men on crucial college admissions tests, such as the Scholastic Aptitude Test, where the gender gap is more than 40 points. The gap costs women admission and scholarship opportunities in the most prestigious colleges and universities.[9]

- Although women comprise 70 percent of students in vocational programs in health, women make up only 28 percent of students in technical vocational programs and 23 percent of students in trade and industry vocational programs.[10]

- Female students confront daily sexual harassment that interferes with their opportunity to learn in an equitable environment. Nearly 80 percent of female students in elementary and secondary schools, and more than 75 percent of female students in colleges and universities report sexual harassment by teachers and peers.[11]

- Women continue to face discrimination in employment in educational institutions. At the elementary and secondary school level, women make up 73 percent of teachers, but only 35 percent of principals, and 10 percent of superintendents.[12]

The persistence of sex discrimination in education demands an examination of the efforts to enforce Title IX in our educational institutions. This report initiated such an investigation into the enforcement efforts of the Office for Civil Rights in the U.S. Department of Education.

Title IX Through the Eyes of Congress and the Courts

In the Congress

The enforcement of Title IX is subject to the mood of the legislature and the legal system. An examination of legislative developments and court rulings reveals substantial threats to efforts to eliminate sex discrimination in education.

Legislative support for the enforcement of Title IX is provided by the Civil Rights Act of 1964, the Women's Educational Equity Act of 1974, the 1976 Amendments to the Vocational Equity Act of 1963, and the Carl D. Perkins Act of 1984.[13]

Title IX is modeled after Title VI of the Civil Rights Act of 1964, which prohibits discrimination on the basis of race, color, and national origin in any program that receives federal financial assistance. Under Title VI and Title IX, the federal government can withhold funds from schools that violate the statutes. ***However, the federal government has never exercised this authority under Title IX.***

Title IV of the Civil Rights Act of 1964 provides support to schools to comply with civil rights laws, including Title IX, by providing funds for regional assistance centers and grants to state education departments for providing more equitable education to students. The support provided for the enforcement of Title IX under Title IV was undermined in 1996, however, by Congress' elimination of state funds for Title IV.[14]

The Women's Educational Equity Act (WEEA), enacted in 1974 under the Elementary and Secondary Education Act, provides federal financial assistance to educational agencies and institutions to meet the requirements of Title IX. This legislation provides funding for programs to improve curriculum and teaching practices to promote gender equity in schools. Federal funding for WEEA came under attack in the House of Representatives in 1999 with the reauthorization of the Elementary and Secondary Education Act. However, Congress voted to maintain funding for WEEA, the only federally funded program devoted exclusively to promoting gender equity in education.

Legislative support for Title IX enforcement also derives from the 1976 Amendments to the Vocational Equity Act of 1963 and the Carl D.

Perkins Act of 1984. The vocational education legislation requires states receiving federal funding to develop and carry out activities to eliminate sex discrimination in vocational education. This legislation also requires states to name state vocational education sex equity coordinators to provide training and produce materials aimed at promoting equity in vocational education.[15] The efforts to enforce Title IX in vocational education were eliminated, however, with the re-authorization of the Carl D. Perkins Act in 1998. During the reauthorization, Congress eliminated the requirement that states fund programs specifically to promote gender equity in vocational education.[16] Furthermore, the Office for Civil Rights no longer requires states to submit reports monitoring the compliance of vocational education programs with civil rights legislation.[17]

In the Courts

The enforcement of Title IX has also been affected by federal court decisions. Decisions by the U.S. Supreme Court determine the extent to which educational institutions are liable for sex discrimination violations under Title IX. The Court's ruling in *Grove City College v. Bell* (1984) had a devastating effect on the enforcement efforts of Title IX: The Court held that Title IX was program-specific (and not institution-wide) in its mandate, and therefore, only those programs and activities that directly received federal funds needed to comply.[18] However, that decision was effectively overturned by the Civil Rights Restoration Act of 1988, which restored liability to an entire educational institution receiving federal funds. Title IX enforcement was further bolstered by the Supreme Court's ruling in *Franklin v. Gwinnett County Public Schools* (1992). The *Franklin* decision increased the potential liability of educational institutions under Title IX by granting students and employees experiencing discrimination the right to sue for monetary damages.[19]

More recent Supreme Court decisions interpreting the law have meant giant steps backward for Title IX enforcement. In *Gebser v. Lago Vista Independent School District* (1998) the Court set strict limits on school districts' liability for teacher-to-student sexual harassment.[20] The Supreme Court had previously held in *Franklin v. Gwinnett County Public Schools* (1992) that sexual harassment is prohibited by Title IX, and that students harmed when schools violate the statute may recover damages from school districts.[21] In the *Gebser* decision, however, the Court narrowed schools' liability by ruling that school districts are not liable for the sexual harassment of students by teachers "unless an official of the school district who at a minimum has authority to institute corrective measures on the district's behalf has **actual notice** of, and is **deliberately indifferent** to, the teacher's misconduct [emphasis added]."[22] The *Gebser* decision so undercuts student protection from teacher sexual harassment that students in schools enjoy less protection from sexual harassment than employees in the workplace.

In two cases decided in the same term as the *Gebser* decision, *Burlington Industries, Inc. v. Ellerth* (1998) and *Faragher v. City of Boca Raton* (1998), the Supreme Court held that businesses regulated under Title VII of the Civil Rights Act of 1964 can be liable for sexual harassment perpetrated by supervisors even if the employer is unaware of the harassment.[23] But the Court ruled that employers are liable only when the harassment results in a tangible employment action (such as hiring, firing, or pay decisions, or when the supervisor uses his or her authority to sexually harass an employee). This standard of protection provides an incentive for employers to actively work to stop sexual harassment. The same standard would also serve to safeguard students in schools and provide similar incentives to educational institutions to stop sexual harassment. Unfortunately, however, the Court rejected application of Title

VII standards to Title IX cases despite the fact that students in an educational environment are often more vulnerable to sexual harassment than adults in the workplace and students are subject to compulsory attendance in schools.

Rather than impose vicarious liability on schools, the Court reiterated the narrower standard of liability for schools under Title IX in *Davis v. Monroe County Board of Education* (1999).[24] Even while expanding Title IX enforcement by confirming that institutions must address student-to-student harassment (an issue about which federal courts and schools were previously uncertain), the *Davis* decision still requires actual notice and deliberate indifference on the part of a school official with authority to institute corrective measures before liability will be imposed.

Without question, *Gebser* and *Davis* make it more difficult to hold school districts liable for sexual harassment under Title IX. These decisions seriously undermine students' ability to seek legal redress against sex discrimination under Title IX. Unless Congress takes action to restore the broad mandate given to Title IX in 1972, the Office for Civil Rights, the primary agency with authority for enforcing Title IX, will remain constrained in its ability to enforce the statute under current interpretations of civil rights law.

The Enforcement of Title IX

The Office for Civil Rights (OCR) in the U.S. Department of Education was established to ensure equal access to education and promote educational excellence throughout the nation through vigorous enforcement of civil rights legislation. As the primary agency responsible for the enforcement of civil rights legislation, OCR monitors compliance with five federal statutes that prohibit discrimination in education programs and activities that receive federal financial assistance:

- Discrimination on the basis of race, color, and national origin is prohibited by Title VI of the Civil Rights Act of 1964.
- Discrimination on the basis of disability is prohibited by Section 504 of the Rehabilitation Act of 1973 and Title II of the Americans With Disabilities Act of 1990.
- Age discrimination is prohibited by the Age Discrimination Act of 1975.
- Sex discrimination is prohibited by Title IX of the Education Amendments of 1972.

Any governmental agency that provides funds to educational programs and activities is authorized to enforce compliance with Title IX. However, OCR assumes primary responsibility for the enforcement of the statute in educational institutions. Title IX protects more than 52 million students attending elementary and secondary schools and more than 14 million students attending colleges and universities. The statute also protects employees of educational institutions receiving federal funds, although OCR refers the vast majority of employment cases to the Equal Employment Opportunity Commission.[25]

OCR regulates Title IX primarily by investigating complaints of illegal sex discrimination filed with the agency. But OCR also enforces the law by conducting compliance reviews and providing technical assistance.

Compliance reviews are independent examinations initiated by OCR. Through such reviews, the agency can, on its own authority, investigate any program or activity of an educational institution receiving federal funds to determine if the program or activity meets Title IX requirements. Even when no complaint has been filed, OCR may initiate an investigation of systemic sex discrimination through a compliance review.

Technical assistance consists of information and advice that OCR dispenses to institutions on request. The assistance is designed to inform institutions of their responsibility under the civil rights statutes and regulations and to help them perform accordingly. OCR provides technical assistance through onsite consultations, conference sponsorship and participation, training classes, community meetings, and the Internet. The agency also provides written and telephone guidance in response to inquiries.

OCR investigates complaints filed with the 12 regional enforcement offices throughout the country. (See Figure 1 and Appendix A.) A complaint may be filed with OCR by anyone who believes that an institution covered by Title IX has discriminated against someone on the basis of sex. A person does not need to be a victim of the alleged discrimination to complain on behalf of another person or group facing sex discrimination. Organizations may also file complaints on behalf of victims of sex discrimination. Title IX protects **both** male and female victims of sex discrimination.[26]

The scope and impact of OCR investigations on the effective enforcement of Title IX is the subject of this report.

Report Methodology

A License for Bias: Sex Discrimination, Schools, and Title IX investigates the Title IX enforcement efforts of the Office for Civil Rights in the U.S. Department of Education. For this report, the AAUW Legal Advocacy Fund reviewed 425 non-sports-related complaints filed with OCR from October 1, 1993, to September 30, 1997. These complaints represented 61 percent of the non-sports-related cases resolved by OCR during the four-year investigation period. Records analyzed included letters of findings, compliance agreements, monitoring letters, and compliance

reviews. The documents were obtained from the national and regional offices of the Office for Civil Rights through requests under the Freedom of Information Act (FOIA). The sample size was limited by difficulties obtaining case information from OCR's regional offices.

OCR received more than 2,000 Title IX cases during the four-year investigation period. The agency assumed responsibility for the investigation of about 1,000 cases, including about 300 cases related to sports and nearly 700 cases related to other areas covered under Title IX.[27]

OCR is not responsible for investigating cases that come under the jurisdiction of another federal agency such as the Equal Employment Opportunity Commission (EEOC). The agency also does not investigate cases pending before a court of law or cases under active investigation through the internal grievance procedures of an educational institution. Once these independent actions have ended, OCR has 60 days to begin its own investigation if there has been no settlement of the complaint allegations. OCR may decide not to investigate complaints that are untimely or deemed completely without merit, or cases in which the complainant does not cooperate with the investigation.[28]

OCR addressed the cases in our sample through four methods of complaint resolution:

- negotiation of an agreement resolving allegations raised prior to the completion of an investigation
- determination of insufficient evidence to support a violation
- negotiation of an agreement based on the results of an investigation
- negotiation of an agreement based on the results of a compliance review[29]

If OCR is unable to achieve voluntary compliance, it can initiate an enforcement action through administrative or judicial proceedings. Enforcement proceedings can result in suspending, terminating, or refusing to grant or continue federal financial aid to the school or college.

Cases resolved through Resolution Between Parties, which involves the facilitation of an agreement directly between the complainant and the institution, were not included in our analysis, as OCR does not maintain files on these cases after resolution.[30] Cases resolved through OCR's initiation of formal enforcement proceedings by the Office for Civil Rights were also not represented in our sample—because there were no such cases. Only cases resolved through formal enforcement can result in the loss of federal funds for educational institutions found in non-compliance with Title IX. *To date, the Office for Civil Rights has never withheld federal funds from an offending institution for violations under Title IX.*[31]

Our investigation of OCR's Title IX enforcement efforts was conducted in two phases. During the first phase, we compiled statistical information about the Title IX cases in our sample along nine characteristics: (1) educa-

Figure 1. Regional Offices of the Office for Civil Rights (1993-1997)		
Region	**Region Covered by Office**	**Regional Office**
Region I	Connecticut, Maine, Massachusetts, New Hampshire, Rhode Island, Vermont	Boston, MA
Region II	New Jersey, New York, Puerto Rico, Virgin Islands	New York, NY
Region III	Delaware, District of Columbia, Maryland, Pennsylvania, Virginia, West Virginia	Philadelphia, PA
Region IV	Alabama, Florida, Georgia, North Carolina, South Carolina, Tennessee	Atlanta, GA
Region V	Illinois, Indiana, Michigan, Minnesota, Ohio, Wisconsin	Chicago, IL
Region VI	Arkansas, Louisiana, Mississippi, Oklahoma, Texas	Dallas, TX
Region VII	Iowa, Kansas, Kentucky,* Missouri, Nebraska	Kansas City, MO
Region VIII	Arizona, Colorado, Montana, New Mexico, North Dakota,* South Dakota,* Utah, Wyoming	Denver, CO
Region IX	California	San Francisco, CA
Region X	Alaska, Hawaii, Idaho, Nevada, Oregon, Washington, American Samoa, Guam, Pacific Islands	Seattle, WA
Region XI**	North Carolina, Virginia, Washington, DC	Washington, DC
Region XV**	Michigan, Ohio	Cleveland, OH

These states were assumed by other existing regional offices during the course of our investigation because of reorganization (Kentucky moved to Region III; North Dakota and South Dakota moved to Region VII).

** These regional offices were created during the course of our investigation as a result of OCR's reorganization.

tional institution, (2) geographical region, (3) year of complaint, (4) level of education, (5) type of complaint, (6) sex of complainant, (7) status of complainant (whether student or staff), (8) length of investigation, and (9) method of resolution of investigation.

During the second phase of investigation, we analyzed OCR's filing, investigation, resolution, and monitoring procedures. This phase identified strengths and weaknesses in OCR's enforcement practices and generated recommendations for improvement. Our report recognizes the progress made toward Title IX enforcement as well as the problems that impede this advancement. We share our findings to spur further progress toward the elimination of sex discrimination in education through the enforcement of Title IX.

Chapter One:
Who's Complaining?

The Office for Civil Rights receives about 5,000 complaints each year, alleging discrimination based on disability, race/national origin, age, and sex. Sex discrimination complaints comprise about 10 percent of complaints filed with the agency. (For a breakdown of all complaints by category, see Figure 2.) About 10 percent of all complaints allege multiple forms of discrimination, including a number of cases involving sex discrimination.[1]

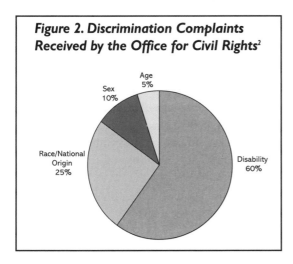

Figure 2. Discrimination Complaints Received by the Office for Civil Rights[2]

To more accurately portray the realities of sex discrimination in education, *A License for Bias* focuses on complaints filed outside athletics. Although the public closely associates Title IX with sports, this emphasis distorts the scope of the law. During the 1993-1997 investigation period, sports-related complaints accounted for less than a third of the 1,000 Title IX cases resolved by OCR.[3]

Case and Complainant Information

Students and employees at all levels of education are protected under the mandate of Title IX. During the investigation period, the Office for Civil Rights resolved slightly more cases of sex discrimination in elementary and secondary education (56 percent) than in higher education (44 percent). *(See Figure 3.)*

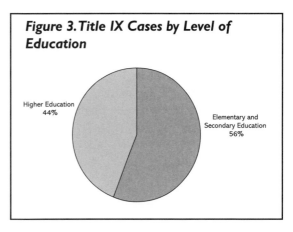

Figure 3. Title IX Cases by Level of Education

Although employees of educational institutions are covered under Title IX, OCR's authority here is limited to the investigation of complaints that allege a pattern and practice of sex discrimination against a group of employees in an institution. OCR generally refers investigation of individual complaints to the EEOC. OCR's limited jurisdiction in employment cases is reflected in the number of cases filed by students and employees under Title IX during the investigation period. Complaints filed by students (or on behalf of students) accounted for 91 percent of sex discrimination cases, while complaints filed by employees accounted for only 9 percent of cases. *(See Figure 4.)*

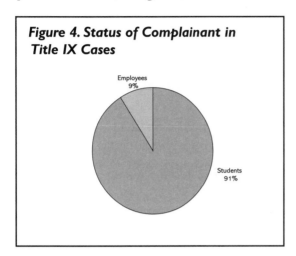

Figure 4. Status of Complainant in Title IX Cases

Title IX protection extends to both females and males. While complaints filed on behalf of females represented the majority (71 percent) of sex discrimination cases, nearly one-third (29 percent) of Title IX cases were filed on behalf of males. *(See Figure 5.)*

Types of Complaints

Title IX prohibits sex discrimination in all areas of education, including admissions and recruitment, educational programs and activities, course offerings, counseling, financial aid, employment assistance, facilities and housing, health and insurance benefits and services, scholarships, athletics, and discrimi-

nation by marital and parental status.[4] During the period of investigation, the five most common complaints of sex discrimination occurred in the areas of (1) sexual harassment, (2) admissions, financial aid, and testing, (3) discipline, (4) procedural requirements, and (5) retaliation.

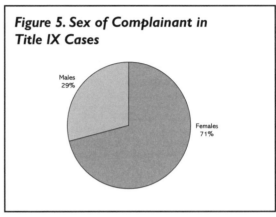

Figure 5. Sex of Complainant in Title IX Cases

Significant patterns emerged when complaints were analyzed by level of education and sex of complainant. Unfair practices in discipline and student treatment were more commonly alleged in elementary and secondary education, while charges of unfair practices in admissions, financial aid, and testing predominated in higher education.

Complaints of sex discrimination filed on behalf of female and male students also differed significantly.

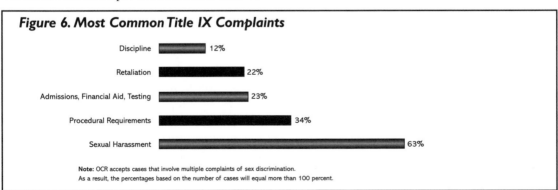

Figure 6. Most Common Title IX Complaints

Discipline 12%
Retaliation 22%
Admissions, Financial Aid, Testing 23%
Procedural Requirements 34%
Sexual Harassment 63%

Note: OCR accepts cases that involve multiple complaints of sex discrimination.
As a result, the percentages based on the number of cases will equal more than 100 percent.

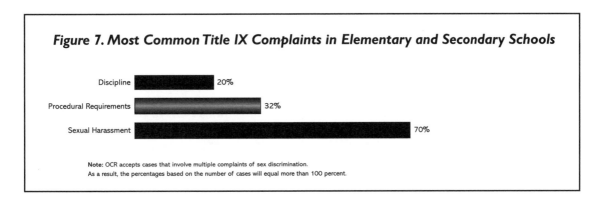

Figure 7. Most Common Title IX Complaints in Elementary and Secondary Schools

Discipline	20%
Procedural Requirements	32%
Sexual Harassment	70%

Note: OCR accepts cases that involve multiple complaints of sex discrimination. As a result, the percentages based on the number of cases will equal more than 100 percent.

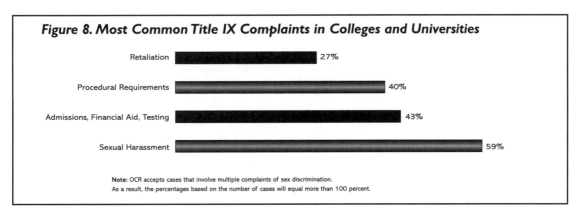

Figure 8. Most Common Title IX Complaints in Colleges and Universities

Retaliation	27%
Procedural Requirements	40%
Admissions, Financial Aid, Testing	43%
Sexual Harassment	59%

Note: OCR accepts cases that involve multiple complaints of sex discrimination. As a result, the percentages based on the number of cases will equal more than 100 percent.

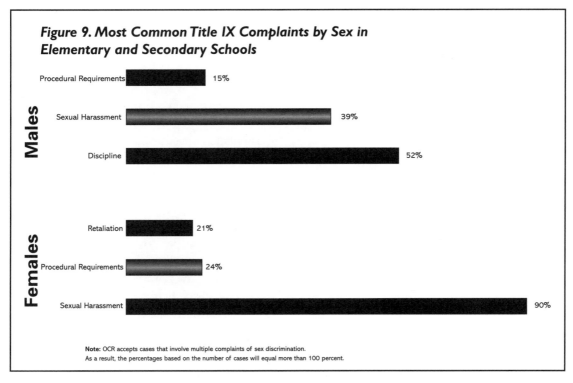

Figure 9. Most Common Title IX Complaints by Sex in Elementary and Secondary Schools

Males

Procedural Requirements	15%
Sexual Harassment	39%
Discipline	52%

Females

Retaliation	21%
Procedural Requirements	24%
Sexual Harassment	90%

Note: OCR accepts cases that involve multiple complaints of sex discrimination. As a result, the percentages based on the number of cases will equal more than 100 percent.

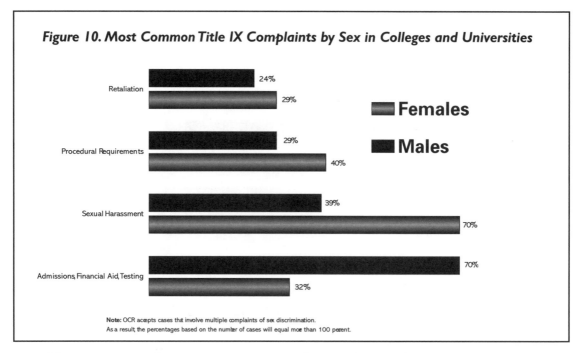

Figure 10. Most Common Title IX Complaints by Sex in Colleges and Universities

- Retaliation — Males: 24%, Females: 29%
- Procedural Requirements — Males: 29%, Females: 40%
- Sexual Harassment — Males: 39%, Females: 70%
- Admissions, Financial Aid, Testing — Males: 70%, Females: 32%

Note: OCR accepts cases that involve multiple complaints of sex discrimination. As a result, the percentages based on the number of cases will equal more than 100 percent.

Sexual harassment was the most pressing concern for female students at all levels of education. Complaints of sexual harassment accounted for 90 percent of sex discrimination cases filed on behalf of female students in elementary and secondary schools, and 70 percent of cases filed on behalf of female students in colleges and universities. In contrast, complaints of sexual harassment accounted for only 39 percent of cases filed on behalf of male students at all educational levels.

More than half of the complaints filed on behalf of male students in elementary and secondary schools involved discrimination in the administration of discipline. Complaints filed on behalf of male students in higher education focused on discrimination in college admissions and evaluation in college courses. Almost half of these complaints involved allegations of discrimination in admissions and retention; nearly one-third alleged discrimination in evaluation and grading in courses.

Compliance Reviews

The Office for Civil Rights regulates civil rights compliance not just through complaint resolution, but also through compliance reviews. The agency initiates compliance reviews to spur adherence to the law in areas that may need further attention such as those areas not represented by complaints.

OCR initiates about 150 compliance reviews each year. However, too few of these focus on sex discrimination in education.[5] During our four-year investigation, regional OCR offices initiated 19 compliance reviews focused on sex discrimination. These reviews made up only 3.2 percent of the approximately 600 compliance reviews initiated by the agency over the four-year span.[6] During the same period, *some regional offices conducted no compliance reviews related to sex discrimination.* Two of the 12 regional offices— Boston and San Francisco—conducted more than half of all compliance reviews related to sex discrimination.

Figure 11. Title IX Sex Discrimination Compliance Reviews by Region		
Regional Office		**Compliance Reviews**
Region Boston Office	I	5
Region New York Office	II	1
Region Philadelphia Office	III	0
Region Atlanta Office	IV	0
Region Chicago Office	V	1
Region Dallas Office	VI	2
Region Kansas City Office	VII	3
Region Denver Office	VIII	0
Region San Francisco Office	IX	6
Region Seattle Office	X	1
Region Washington DC Office	XI	0
Region Cleveland Office	XV	0
Total		**19**

elementary and secondary schools these issues include unfair practices in the administration of discipline. In colleges and universities, awarding admissions and scholarships on the basis of standardized test scores and segregating the sexes by field of study similarly demand scrutiny. At all levels of education, OCR should initiate compliance reviews to determine whether educational institutions have met Title IX procedural requirements by appointing an equity coordinator and establishing grievance procedures.

The recommendation to initiate more compliance reviews must consider OCR's limited time, funding, and staff resources. However, we suggest that the percentage of compliance reviews on issues of sex discrimination be at least proportionate to the percentage of sex discrimination complaints filed with the agency each year. During our four-year investigation, while sex discrimination complaints comprised 10 percent of OCR's caseload, only 3.2 percent of compliance reviews initiated by the agency focused on sex discrimination.[7]

Compliance reviews initiated by the regional offices focused on the incidence of sexual harassment in schools, the underrepresentation of girls and women in mathematics and science, and the access and quality of vocational education available to girls and women. Our analysis of sex discrimination complaints during the investigation period reveals other problem areas that warrant greater attention. In

Chapter Two:
Trends and Issues in Title IX Complaints

An examination of sex discrimination complaints by category reveals important differences in filing and handling patterns and, consequently, in the degree of protection enjoyed by individuals concerned with those areas. The chief categories of complaint we examined are sexual harassment; admissions, financial aid, and testing; discipline; participation in nontraditional fields; and sex discrimination against employees.

Sexual Harassment

The widespread nature of sexual harassment in schools has been well established since a 1993 study showed that four out of every five students has experienced some form of the problem.[1] The study further revealed the prevalence of sexual harassment of students by employees, with 25 percent of girls and 10 percent of boys reporting abuses by school faculty and staff.[2] Sexual harassment of students by peers is even more extensive, with nearly 80 percent of students reporting harassment by another student.[3] Female students, in particular, can expect to face sexual harassment from grade school to graduate school. Sexual harassment affects nearly 80 percent of girls in elementary and secondary schools, more than 75 percent of women in colleges and universities, and at least 50 percent of women in the workplace.[4] Female students also face more frequent and more severe sexual harassment than male students,[5] including sexual assault and rape.[6] Female students also suffer greater problems as a consequence of sexual harassment.[7]

Sexual harassment in school can have a profoundly negative effect on a student's education.

The physical and emotional damage inflicted by sexual harassment can shatter self-esteem, thereby causing a student to lose confidence in the ability to succeed in school.[8] Sexual harassment limits a student's opportunity to receive an equitable education.

Sexual Harassment as a Form of Sex Discrimination

Under the guidelines established by OCR, sexual harassment is a form of sex discrimination prohibited under Title IX of the Education Amendments of 1972. The regulation implementing Title IX at 34 C.F.R. Section 106.31 outlaws sexual harassment as a form of disparate treatment that impedes access to an equitable education. Sexual harassment of students—both male and female—by school employees, students, and others (such as athletes visiting the school) is illegal under Title IX. Title IX prohibits sexual harassment when the harasser and target of the harassment are of the same gender if the misconduct is based on the gender of the target.[9] Students are protected under Title IX from sexual harassment in all school programs and activities, whether they take place in the school, on a school bus, or at a program sponsored by the school at another location.[10]

OCR identifies two types of sexual harassment in schools, quid pro quo and hostile environment. Quid pro quo sexual harassment occurs when a school employee causes a student to believe that he or she must submit to unwelcome sexual conduct to participate in a school program or activity such as student council. It can also occur when a teacher suggests to a student that an educational decision such as grades will be based on whether or not the student submits to unwelcome sexual conduct. Hostile environment harassment occurs when unwelcome verbal or physical conduct is sufficiently severe, persistent, or pervasive that it creates an abusive or hostile environment from the perspective of the affected student. To rise to the level of harassment, a one-time incident must be severe enough to warrant notification of legal authorities as in the case of attempted sexual assault or rape.[11]

According to OCR guidelines, the following behaviors constitute sexual harassment:

- sexual advances
- touching of a sexual nature
- graffiti of a sexual nature
- displaying or distributing of sexually explicit drawings, pictures, and written materials
- sexual gestures and sexual jokes
- pressure for sexual favors
- touching oneself sexually or talking about one's sexual activity in front of others
- spreading rumors about or rating other students' sexual activity or performance[12]

"Unwelcomeness" is the determining factor in assessing whether a sexual behavior is considered sexual harassment. Flirtation and other sexual advances are not considered harassment if they are welcome. To determine whether the sexual conduct is welcome, the degree of influence of the alleged harasser over the student should be assessed along with other factors such as the history of the alleged harasser. Classroom discussions and materials with sexual content do not constitute sexual harassment when consistent with the educational purpose of the course. However, derogatory language targeting girls and women in the classroom creates a hostile environment that constitutes sexual harassment.[13]

To adequately address sexual harassment, institutions must develop sex discrimination policies that include sexual harassment. The OCR guidelines on sexual harassment suggest that school policies

- give notice of sexual harassment policies and procedures, including where complaints can be filed, to students, parents, and employees
- assign an investigator to the complainant and give parties involved the opportunity to present witnesses and evidence
- set time frames for the process and give all parties involved notice of the outcome
- give assurance that the school will take steps to prevent recurrence of the harassment and to correct the negative effects of the harassment on affected students
- ensure that the response does not penalize the victim of harassment
- prevent retaliation against the complainant by other students and employees[14]

A student who experiences harassment should file a claim with school officials, including the principal, school board members, superintendent, and Title IX coordinator. Filing a claim with these officials helps ensure that students will meet the actual notice standards as defined by the Supreme Court. Students and their parents can also file a claim with OCR.

Sexual Harassment Complaints

Our investigation revealed that sexual harassment was the most prevalent form of discrimination against which complainants sought Title IX protection. Nearly two-thirds of all Title IX cases we investigated involved complaints of sexual harassment. More than half of these sexual harassment cases alleged harassment of students by teachers and faculty. About one-third of students' sexual harassment complaints involved harassment by peers. Complaints of sexual harassment were more prevalent in elementary and secondary schools (where they accounted for 70 percent of complaints) than colleges and universities (59 percent of complaints), although the problem was pervasive at all levels of education.

The incidence of sexual harassment was greatest for female students, particularly in elementary and secondary schools. There, harassment complaints accounted for 90 percent of sex discrimination cases filed on behalf of female students. In colleges and universities, 70 percent of cases filed on behalf of female students concerned sexual harassment. In contrast, sexual harassment complaints accounted for only 39 percent of cases filed on behalf of male students at both the elementary/secondary school level and in higher education. Girls and women in schools and universities seeking protection from sexual harassment by faculty and peers accounted for more than three-fourths of all sexual harassment complaints. Girls represented more than 80 percent of complainants in sexual harassment cases in ele-

mentary and secondary schools, and women represented more than 70 percent of complainants in sexual harassment cases in colleges and universities.

Institutional Policies and Procedures on Sexual Harassment

Our investigation also revealed that more than one-third of sex discrimination cases involved complaints against institutions for failing to meet the procedural requirements under Title IX. Among the violations charged were failures to establish grievance procedures, appoint a designated representative, and publish public notices of nondiscrimination. A majority of these complaints were filed in connection with sexual harassment complaints. More than 20 percent of sex discrimination cases involved complaints of retaliation for filing a sexual harassment complaint under Title IX. These patterns indicate a widespread failure of schools and universities to adequately address incidents of sexual harassment.

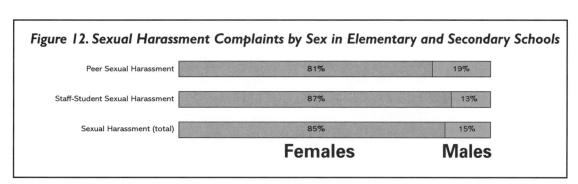

Figure 12. Sexual Harassment Complaints by Sex in Elementary and Secondary Schools

Peer Sexual Harassment — 81% / 19%
Staff-Student Sexual Harassment — 87% / 13%
Sexual Harassment (total) — 85% / 15%

Females — Males

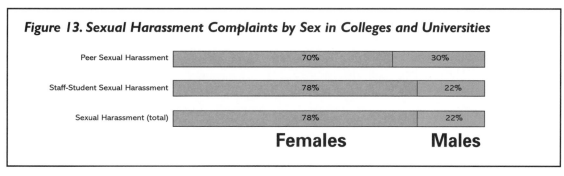

Figure 13. Sexual Harassment Complaints by Sex in Colleges and Universities

Peer Sexual Harassment — 70% / 30%
Staff-Student Sexual Harassment — 78% / 22%
Sexual Harassment (total) — 78% / 22%

Females — Males

Although U.S. law requires all schools and universities to establish grievance procedures for addressing sex discrimination, including sexual harassment, many institutions do not comply with Title IX in this respect. A 1993 survey by the Wellesley Center for Research on Women and NOW Legal Defense and Education Fund found that only 8 percent of elementary and secondary schools had created and enforced a sex discrimination policy that addresses sexual harassment. The study also found that schools without sexual harassment policies were much less likely to act in sexual harassment cases. Schools with sexual harassment policies took action in 84 percent of cases; schools without such policies acted on only 52 percent of cases.[15]

Case Studies: Schools' Failure to Address Sexual Harassment

Our investigation revealed the persistent and pervasive problem of sexual harassment against female students in schools. Starting early in grade school, female students were subjected to sexual harassment and abuse at school. Consider these examples:

- A group of five first grade girls in Madison, Wisconsin, was harassed by a group of 20 second grade boys on the school playground. The boys chased the girls every day at recess and forced the girls to kiss and touch them in a sexual way.

- A boy assaulted a girl in kindergarten in Aiken, South Carolina. The boy asked the girl to "see her panties" and attempted to place his hands inside her underwear. When she tried to get away from him, he kicked and choked her. The girl suffered bruises on her neck, wrists, and ankles.

Female students from grade school to graduate school filed complaints with OCR alleging sexual harassment from male students and teachers. Complainants sought protection from the agency because their schools were largely unresponsive to the problem. In many cases, the schools failed to investigate the charges; often, schools did not even have policies and procedures on how to conduct such an investigation. When the schools did respond, they often failed to resolve the incident and provide an appropriate remedy. These cases are representative:

- A high school in Terrel, Texas, failed to act when a female student complained that she was repeatedly harassed by a group of male students. In frustration, the student dropped out of school.

- A high school in Lawndale, California, failed to act when a female student complained of sexual harassment by a male teacher. The year after she complained to administrators, the school again assigned her to the same teacher.

- A high school in Idaho City, Idaho, failed to provide an appropriate remedy for a female student who was sexually harassed by a male teacher. In response to the harassment, the school removed the student from the teacher's class and arranged for her to complete the course through independent study. However, the school gave the student no access to instruction during the independent study and did not monitor her performance. The school, in effect, retaliated against the complainant by failing to provide her with an equitable learning environment.

- A high school in Orting, Washington, failed to protect three female students from repeated harassment by a male student who verbally and physically harassed them over the course of an entire school year. Despite frequent school detentions and suspensions, he continued to target them; he even harassed them on the day he returned from a suspension. The school took no further actions. The female students could not file a complaint with the school because the school did not have any procedures for investigating sexual harassment complaints.

- A high school in Monroe, Oregon, failed to provide an appropriate remedy for female students who complained of a sexually hostile environment from male students at the school. In response to complaints, the principal made presentations to the students about sexual harassment. In the presentation for male students, the principal said, "Just because a girl is friendly, it does not mean that she is inviting sexual overtures from you." He also told the male students to "keep their hands off the girls." In the presentation for the female students, the principal told the audience, "Be aware of how your actions could lead to sexual overtures by the boys." The principal did not use the presentations to provide written materials about the school's policies and procedures for complaints of sexual harassment.

The inaction (or wrong actions) of these schools denied female students their right to an equitable education as mandated under Title IX.

OCR Investigations of Sexual Harassment

OCR investigates complaints of sexual harassment by determining whether the incidents occurred as alleged by the complainant and whether the inappropriate conduct was sufficiently severe, persistent, or pervasive to be considered sexual harassment. The agency also reviews whether the school had notice of the harassment and conducted an investigation into the incidents of sexual harassment.

However, OCR's investigations of sexual harassment complaints can be impeded by the investigative practices of the agency. OCR relies on witnesses to determine whether an alleged incident has occurred; however, there are often no witnesses to such incidents. When there are witnesses, they are often reluctant to be interviewed for fear of retaliation from other students. The victim may also be reluctant to discuss the incidents because of fear and embarrassment. Consider these cases:

- A female student in a Henderson, Texas, middle school did not report an incident of sexual harassment on the school bus in which a male student slapped her on the buttocks and pinched her breasts. She was too embarrassed to discuss the incident with the principal and did not feel that the principal would take action against the male student. OCR learned of the incident through another student who cited it to support her complaint that the school district had accepted a hostile environment.

- A group of female students at a high school in Monroe, Oregon, initially did not report repeated harassment from male students at the school because they feared the perpetrators and felt humiliated. Eventually, OCR received a complaint. During OCR's investigation, a teacher noted that female students are often too uncomfortable and embarrassed to report sexual harassment.

In many cases, OCR did not find sufficient evidence to support complaints of sexual harassment. However, the agency usually found evidence that the schools lacked policies and procedures to address complaints of sexual harassment. The agency then negotiated an agreement with the schools to remedy their violations of Title IX.

Some of the remedies stipulated in the agreements include the following:

- Schools must develop and distribute sex discrimination policies that include sexual harassment as a form of sex discrimination under Title IX. Schools must develop and implement grievance procedures for investigating and resolving complaints of sexual harassment. Schools must also develop student codes of conduct that include disciplinary actions for students who sexually harass other students.

- Schools must appoint a Title IX coordinator to investigate and resolve sex discrimination complaints.

- Schools must provide training for faculty, staff, and students about school policies and procedures on sexual harassment.

- Schools must conduct surveys and collect information on the incidence of sexual harassment at the school. They must record information on student complaints of sexual harassment and the school's investigation of such complaints. Schools must provide this information to OCR during the monitoring of the compliance agreement.

- Schools must discipline employees for sexually harassing students; schools may terminate employees for harassment. Schools must discipline students for sexually harassing other students; schools may provide counseling and training to students who harass other students.

- Schools must provide remedies such as counseling for the victim of harassment.

Our findings suggest that OCR's investigation of sexual harassment complaints will not be enough to end this pervasive problem. Schools must implement policies and procedures to protect students from sexual harassment and train teachers and students about sexual harassment.

Admissions, Financial Aid, and Testing

The Use of Standardized Tests in College Admissions and Financial Aid Decisions

Title IX prohibits sex discrimination in college admissions and scholarship decisions. Colleges and universities have a legal responsibility to employ practices that ensure equal access to opportunities in higher education. Many schools, however, base admissions and scholarship decisions largely on college admissions test scores. Reliance on these test scores compromises equitable access to educational opportunities in colleges and universities.

Overall, female students score lower than male students on college admissions tests (for example, girls underscore boys by more than 40 points on the Scholastic Aptitude Test).[16] Overall, female students also score lower than male students on the Advanced Placement and Achievement tests in subjects such as mathematics, chemistry, physics, and biology; these tests are crucial for admission to the most selective colleges and universities.[17]

By itself, a gender gap in college admissions test scores does not necessarily indicate sex discrimination. What makes college admissions tests discriminatory is the fact that male and female students with the same ability levels (as measured by grades) obtain different scores.[18] A female student in high school with an A+ grade point average can expect to score more than 80 points lower on college admissions tests than her male counterpart.[19] In addition, these standardized tests do not accurately predict college success. Instead, college admissions tests tend to underpredict the success of females and overpredict the success of males in college (as measured by college grades).[20]

The use of the college admissions tests for

admissions and scholarship decisions, then, constitutes a form of discrimination declared illegal under Title IX.

Sex Discrimination in Admissions, Financial Aid, and Testing

Title IX prohibits sex discrimination in admissions to all vocational, professional, graduate, and public undergraduate institutions. Title IX does not apply to admissions to private undergraduate institutions, including military schools, or to public and private primary and secondary schools. However, institutions exempt from Title IX admissions requirements must still protect students and employees from sex discrimination in discipline, retaliation, and other areas of education. According to the regulations implementing Title IX at 34 C.F.R. Section 106.21-106.23, educational institutions receiving federal funds may not employ the following admissions practices:

- prefer applicants of one sex by ranking applicants separately by sex
- apply limitations on the number or proportion of persons of either sex who may be admitted to the institution
- use tests that have a disproportionately adverse impact on the basis of sex, unless the test is shown to accurately predict success in the educational program and unless alternative tests or criteria without a disproportionately adverse impact are not available

- treat male and female applicants differently based on parental, family, or marital status
- discriminate on the basis of sex in the recruitment of students

Educational institutions may employ some of these practices, however, in the interest of remedying past sex discrimination.

Title IX also requires colleges and universities to employ equitable practices in awarding scholarships and financial aid. Under the regulations implementing Title IX at C.F.R. Section 106.37, institutions may not

- provide different amounts or types of financial assistance on the basis of sex
- limit eligibility for financial assistance on the basis of sex
- apply different eligibility standards for financial assistance on the basis of sex
- employ students in a way that discriminates on the basis of sex

There are exceptions under which institutions may award financial assistance on the basis of sex (such as for compensatory purposes to remedy past discrimination) as long as the overall effect of the distribution of these funds does not discriminate on the basis of sex. This exception, however, has often been used to continue to provide scholarships exclusively to male students, even in fields that have high rates of male participation.[21]

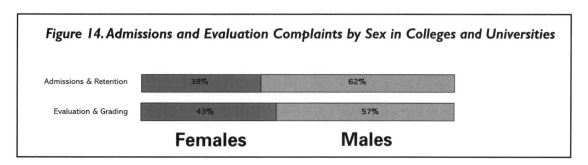

Figure 14. Admissions and Evaluation Complaints by Sex in Colleges and Universities

	Females	Males
Admissions & Retention	38%	62%
Evaluation & Grading	43%	57%

Admissions, Financial Aid, and Testing Complaints

Our research revealed that complaints of discrimination in admissions, financial aid, and testing represented more than 20 percent of Title IX cases filed with OCR. This category of complaints includes admissions, enrollment, retention, dismissal, testing, evaluation, and financial aid. Complaints filed in these areas accounted for 43 percent of sex discrimination cases filed on behalf of college students. These complaints, however, did not adequately address the problem of standardized testing in college admissions and scholarship decisions.

Most complaints of discrimination in college admissions, financial aid, and testing and evaluation were filed on behalf of male college students. Almost half the complaints filed by male college students alleged discrimination in admissions and retention. Nearly one-third of the complaints filed by male college students alleged discrimination in course evaluation and grading.

The basis for most male college student complaints in admissions, financial aid, and testing was the claim that colleges and universities gave illegal preference to females and people of color. None of these complaints was substantiated by the evidence in the OCR investigations.

Case Studies: OCR Enforcement Action on the Misuse of Standardized Tests

During the period covered by our investigation, sex discrimination in the use of standardized testing in college admissions and scholarship decisions was addressed by the Office for Civil Rights in a major case against the College Entrance Examination Board (College Board) and the Educational Testing Service (ETS).

In 1994 the National Center for Fair & Open Testing (FairTest) filed a complaint with OCR alleging sex discrimination against female students in the development and administration of the Preliminary Scholastic Aptitude Test/National Merit Scholarship Qualifying Test (PSAT/NMSQT). The prestigious National Merit Scholarship is awarded based on student scores on the Preliminary Scholastic Aptitude Test (PSAT) taken by high school sophomores and juniors. The scholarship competition awards almost $30 million to students each year.

In the complaint, FairTest alleged that female students score lower than male students on both the verbal and mathematics sections of the PSAT, although female students earn higher grades than male students in high school and college. This allegation provided evidence of test bias since female students and male students with the same ability (as measured by grades) obtain different scores on the test.[22] FairTest also alleged that although less than half the students taking the test are male, males receive nearly two-thirds of the scholarships each year. OCR found evidence of a Title IX violation in the use of the PSAT to award the scholarship to students. The agency determined that the use of the test has a disproportionately adverse impact on female students.

In 1996 OCR negotiated a compliance agreement with the College Board and ETS that required them to develop a new multiple-choice "writing" section for the PSAT. Female students have outscored male students on this writing section, and, as a result, female students have narrowed the gap in test scores by 40 percent.[23] Nonetheless, female students still earn about 1,000 scholarships fewer than they deserve (based on grades and other qualifications) at a loss of $2 million in the National Merit Scholarship competition each year.[24]

OCR's enforcement action in this case has important implications for addressing sex discrimination in the use of the Scholastic Aptitude Test (SAT) and the Graduate Record Exam (GRE), for which there is also extensive evidence of test bias.[25]

Discipline
Problems in Elementary and Secondary Schools

Title IX's promise to ensure an equitable education extends to both male and female students. Both boys and girls face issues in academics and discipline that compromise their access to an equitable education. In terms of academics, boys receive lower report card grades and are more likely to repeat grades and drop out of school.[26] Boys are also the majority of students identified for special education.[27] In terms of discipline, boys experience more difficulty adjusting to school and are more likely to engage in misbehavior there.[28] Boys' misbehavior results in harsh penalties, including corporal punishment. Boys comprise more than 70 percent of students receiving school suspensions and more than 80 percent of students receiving corporal punishment.[29] Boys of color receive the most severe punishments for misbehavior in schools. Although they represent fewer than 10 percent of the student population, they comprise more than 20 percent of students receiving school suspensions and nearly 30 percent of students receiving corporal punishment.[30] Furthermore, boys receive harsher punishments than girls (with boys of color receiving the harshest punishments) even for a similar offense.[31]

Sex Discrimination in the Administration of Discipline

Sex discrimination in the administration of discipline is a form of disparate treatment prohibited by Title IX at 34 C.F.R. Section 106.31. The regulations at Section 106.31(b) state that schools cannot "subject any person to separate or different rules of behavior, sanctions, or other treatment" on the basis of sex. Despite the severity of this problem in elementary and secondary schools, OCR has not issued further policy guidance. We recommend that the agency develop guidelines to deal more appropriately with this problem in order to ensure an equitable learning environment for girls and boys in our schools.

Disciplinary Complaints

Complaints involving the administration of discipline represented 12 percent of Title IX cases. Allegations of unfair disciplinary practices were more common in elementary and secondary schools, where they represented 20 percent of discrimination cases. At this level, the problem was a greater concern for male students, particularly male students of color. More than half the complaints filed by male students in elementary and secondary schools involved discipline. Boys represented 65 percent of the complainants in such cases. Although statistics were not systematically collected on race in sex discrimination cases, an examination of the case files indicated that boys of color were noticeably overrepresented among complainants in discipline cases.

Figure 15. Discipline Complaints by Sex in Elementary and Secondary Schools

Case Studies: Gender, Race, and Discipline in Schools

During the period covered by our investigation, OCR investigated 48 cases of sex discrimination in the administration of discipline. The cases involving discipline were mostly filed by the parents of boys of color in elementary and secondary schools. Complaints of sex and race discrimination were investigated by OCR under Title VI of the Civil Rights Act of 1964 and Title IX of the Educational Amendments of 1972. Some sample cases:

- The mother of an African American male student in a Dallas, Texas, middle school alleged that her son was excessively punished for his misbehavior at school. The student was punished with in-school suspension—removal from regular academic classes—for two days for talking in the cafeteria. The student was also removed from science class for talking and was punished with two days of out-of-school suspension for being rude and disrespectful in math class.

- The father of a Hispanic male student in a high school in Poteet, Texas, alleged that his son was punished more severely than a white female student was for leaving the school grounds without permission during the school day. The male student received two days of on-campus suspension while the female student received a verbal reprimand for the incident.

- The mother of an African American male student in a San Antonio, Texas, middle school alleged that her son was punished more harshly than other students at his school. For pushing another male student and injuring his arm, the student was punished with five days in an alternative placement program. The mother cited another incident in which a white female student was punished with only an in-school suspension for an incident in which she injured a student.

OCR Investigations of Discrimination in the Administration of Discipline

OCR investigates complaints of discrimination in the administration of discipline by reviewing the disciplinary policies and procedures of the school and by reviewing the school's investigation of the incident. The agency determines whether the school has established guidelines for administering discipline to students based on the seriousness of the offense and the frequency of misbehavior by the student. It then determines whether the school handled the incident of misbehavior appropriately and according to established policy and practice at the school. OCR then compares the sanctions placed on the student involved in the incident with sanctions for similar offenses at the school to determine whether the school discriminated. In all cases profiled in this section, OCR found that the sanctions were within the school's guidelines and were comparable to sanctions assigned to similarly situated students (white and female) in the school.

During the period of our investigation, most male student complaints (65 percent) involving discrimination in the administration of discipline were not substantiated by the evidence. Although most disciplinary complaints filed by male students were not substantiated by OCR, the issue of alleged discrimination in the administration of discipline remains a complicated problem for schools—one that demonstrates the complexities of issues of gender and race in our schools. When, for example, a Decatur, Illinois, school imposed a two-year suspension on a group of African American male students in 1999 for fighting at a school event, the Rev. Jesse Jackson and others complained the students received harsh punishment because of their race. The incident underscores some of the difficulties for schools in meting out discipline.

We recommend that OCR initiate compliance reviews to investigate the problem of alleged discrimination against male students of color in the administration of discipline.

Participation in Nontraditional Fields

Underrepresentation of Female Students

Despite the progress made over the last three decades, girls and women continue to be denied equal access to some areas of education, particularly in the traditionally male fields and disciplines of mathematics, science, and engineering. Girls' relative lack of preparation in these fields translates into economic losses for women when they enter the competitive job market, thus creating a barrier for the progress of women in society.

At the secondary level there has been some progress toward the increased participation of girls in nontraditional fields such as mathematics and science. Girls have nearly closed the course-taking gender gap in mathematics and science; however, girls continue to participate at lower levels than boys do in physics and computer science courses.[32] Girls also continue to score well below boys on the mathematics section of college admissions tests such as the SAT.[33] Such disparities discourage girls from pursuing an undergraduate degree in the sciences, as well as graduate study and employment in these fields after college graduation.

At the college level, where women represent more than half the students, they continue to be underrepresented in nontraditional fields such as mathematics, science, and engineering. While women earn 75 percent of undergraduate degrees in education and 69 percent of degrees in psychology, they earn only 28 per-

cent of degrees in computer science.[34] The percentage of women earning graduate degrees in science and engineering is even smaller. In engineering, women earn 16 percent of undergraduate degrees and 15 percent of master's degrees, but only 9 percent of doctoral degrees.[35] Those women who do persist in nontraditional fields often face hostility from male students and faculty and receive only limited support because of the lack of female faculty in these areas.[36]

In vocational education, virtually no progress has been made toward the participation of girls and women in nontraditional fields. Although women are no longer prohibited from taking courses in technical fields, as they were before Title IX, vocational programs still segregate women in traditionally female fields. Women continue to be relegated to lower-paying fields of study in health and clerical programs, while men continue to dominate higher-skill and higher-paying professions in trade and industry, technology, and engineering programs.[37] While women accounted for 70 percent of students in health programs, they represented only 28 percent of students in technical programs and 23 percent of students in trade and industry programs.[38] These disparities exist in vocational programs in high schools and community colleges.

Considerable economic losses for girls and women result from their unequal participation in nontraditional fields of mathematics, science, and engineering. Women in nontraditional careers earn 20 percent to 30 percent more than women in traditional careers.[39] Educational policies and practices that segregate girls and women into lower-status and lower-paying fields and disciplines in educational institutions constitute a form of sex discrimination prohibited by Title IX.

Increasing Female Participation in Nontraditional Fields

Stepping up the participation of girls and women in nontraditional fields is the goal of regulations implementing Title IX in three areas: courses, counseling, and recruitment. The regulations set the following rules:

Courses (Sections 106.34-106.35)

- Educational institutions may not teach students separately on the basis of sex (except to remedy previous sex discrimination).

- Institutions may not mandate participation in a course, including vocational and technical education courses, on the basis of sex and may not exclude a student on the basis of sex.

- Institutions must identify courses that have disproportionate enrollment by sex and investigate whether such enrollment is the result of sex discrimination.

Counseling (Section 106.36)

- Educational institutions may not discriminate on the basis of sex in counseling students for course selection and career planning.

- Counseling materials such as interest inventories and pamphlets must not contain sex bias such that the use of such materials results in disproportionate enrollments in courses and programs.

Recruitment (Sections 106.21-106.23)

- Educational institutions must make comparable efforts to recruit students of each sex for courses and programs.

- Institutions must recruit underrepresented students to remedy the effects of past discrimination.

Institutions must also ensure that female students do not face a hostile environment from sexual harassment in courses and programs in which there are few female students and faculty. These regulations are intended to ensure the equal participation of girls and women in nontraditional fields in educational institutions.

Complaints Concerning the Underrepresentation of Female Students in Nontraditional Fields

The underrepresentation of female students in nontraditional fields was not indicated by complaints filed with the Office for Civil Rights during our investigation period. Instead, the problem was addressed through 15 compliance reviews initiated by the agency. OCR focused compliance reviews on the following:

- participation of female students in mathematics and science courses in high schools (eight reviews)

- participation of female students in vocational education programs (three reviews)

- admission of female students to engineering programs in colleges and universities (four reviews)

To determine whether female students were enrolled in mathematics and science courses in proportion to their numbers in the school population, the agency examined enrollment data provided by the schools under review. OCR found female students adequately represented in mathematics and science courses; however, the agency found minority students significantly underrepresented. The agency did not examine the intersection of race and sex to determine if minority female students (or minority male students) were underrepresented. The agency's findings are consistent with research that demonstrates the increased participation of female students in mathematics and science courses in high schools.

In vocational education, however, OCR found a less equitable course distribution. Female students in the vocational schools under review were concentrated in traditional programs for women such as early childhood education, health occupations, and fashion. Male students were concentrated in traditional programs for men such as engineering, technology, and industry. The agency found that continued bias in counseling and recruitment contributes to the underrepresentation of female students in nontraditional program areas. For example, OCR found that guidance counselors in vocational schools endorsed stereotypes about the interests and abilities of female students and used biased materials when recruiting students. The counselors made no attempt to recruit female students to nontraditional programs.

OCR also found that female students in nontraditional programs were subjected to sexual harassment from male teachers and peers and were often denied access to adequate facilities such as restrooms and locker rooms. These vocational school conditions contributed to a hostile environment for female students. OCR negotiated agreements with the vocational schools to improve the recruitment and participation of female students in nontraditional programs and to improve the experiences of female students in vocational education.

OCR also focused compliance reviews on the admission of female students to mathematics, science, and engineering programs in colleges and universities. Here, the agency examined applicant data at the schools under review to determine whether female students were admitted to the programs in numbers proportionate to their representation in the pool of applicants. The agency also reviewed admissions criteria

(grade point average, standardized test scores, and high school transcripts) to determine whether the criteria adversely affected female students at these schools.

OCR found that gender disparities continue in admissions to mathematics, science, and engineering programs. In science, male students represented more than 80 percent of students admitted. However, the agency did not find the disparities constituted a violation of Title IX. Instead, the agency concluded that female students were admitted to the programs in numbers proportionate to their representation in the applicant pool. In fact, female applicants were admitted at higher rates than male applicants were, with 85 percent of male applicants and nearly 95 percent of female applicants gaining admission. While fewer females applied, those who did were judged more qualified than male applicants based on the admissions criteria. The agency also found that female students had higher rates of retention and graduation from science programs.

Although OCR did not consider the institutions to be in noncompliance regarding the enrollment of female students in science programs, the agency missed an opportunity to negotiate agreements to increase the recruitment of female students into these programs.

Case Studies: Making a "PATH" for Female Participation in Vocational Education

The Office for Civil Rights initiated a compliance review into the participation of female students in a vocational education program at the Portland Arts and Technology High School (PATHS) in Portland, Maine. The PATHS review was prompted by reports that the school had an inadequate enrollment of female students in the program, particularly within nontraditional vocational program areas. Such disproportionate enrollment patterns by sex are common in most vocational schools in the country.

The agency found that male students outnumbered female students by nearly three to one. No female students were enrolled in areas such as auto technology, carpentry, masonry, and welding. Male students were disproportionately concentrated in program areas related to technology (where they represented 96 percent of enrollment) and industry (where they accounted for 90 percent of enrollment). Female students were disproportionately concentrated in program areas related to education (with 87 percent of enrollment), health (with 88 percent of enrollment), and service (with 89 percent of enrollment). Only a few program areas such as data processing had roughly equal numbers of female and male students. The agency found that out of the 23 program areas offered, 19 had predominantly male enrollments.

OCR found sex bias in the counseling and recruitment of female students in nontraditional program areas at the school. The agency found that guidance counselors endorsed stereotypes about the interests of female students in the program and made discriminatory statements such as "young ladies don't like to do the dirty or heavy work" involved in electricity and welding. Counselors openly discouraged some female students from entering nontraditional fields such as auto mechanics and used biased recruiting materials, including a video with content OCR found offensive to female students.

OCR found that counselors also discriminated by recommending students to the program who were "floundering" and were "not solid college track" or had "no apparent goals." Counselors often referred students in need of special education to the vocational education program; almost half of the students enrolled at PATHS were found to be students with special educational needs. By placing such students in the program, counselors may have also discriminated against male students (who are disproportionately referred for special education) and against female students who were not identified for the vocational education program.

OCR also found that female students in nontraditional programs in the school were subjected to constant sexual harassment from male teachers and peers. Female students in program areas such as auto mechanics reported that they were "taunted, teased, and ostracized" by male peers. A female student said that she transferred from plumbing to fashion after repeated harassment. The pervasive problem of sexual harassment in the school contributed to a hostile environment for female students in the program. Similarly, male students in nontraditional programs such as childcare also reported being taunted and teased by other students in the program.

In September 1996 OCR negotiated a compliance agreement with the school to create a "path" for female vocational education students. Under the terms of the agreement, the school has developed a five-year plan to increase the participation of female students in nontraditional vocational education programs. The school plans to use funds from a gender equity grant to provide training for students, teachers, and guidance counselors about opportunities for female students in nontraditional fields. The school also plans to seek additional funding to produce a recruitment video aimed at potential female students in vocational education and to develop a recruitment program for female middle school students. The school also plans to develop another vocational program area to attract equal numbers of male and female students to the school.

OCR's finding of discrimination and bias in PATHS has implications for the participation of female students in vocational education programs in secondary schools throughout the country. OCR should make efforts to disseminate its findings in cases that could impact the Title IX enforcement in our schools and universities.

Discrimination Against Employees in Educational Institutions

The Status of Female Employees in Educational Institutions

Although education is considered a female-dominated profession, women face considerable discrimination as employees in educational institutions. Women faculty and administrators at all levels of education experience unequal treatment in salaries, benefits, and promotions. Many women teachers and professors also experience hostile work environments as a result of sexual harassment from their colleagues and supervisors. Discrimination against female employees in educational institutions is prohibited by law under Title IX.

The unequal status of women as employees in elementary and secondary education is evident in patterns of teacher salaries. Even though women are the majority of teachers in elementary and secondary schools, they earn considerably less than their male counterparts. While male teachers earn an average of $41,000 a year, female teachers earn only $35,000.[40] Male teachers also earn almost twice as much as female teachers in supplemental income from coaching and other activities.[41]

The unequal status of women in the education profession is further evident in patterns of promotion. Although women make up 73 percent of teachers in elementary and secondary schools, they account for only 35 percent of principals and less than 15 percent of superintendents.[42] Not only are more men promoted to positions as school administrators, they are promoted with fewer years of service than women who attain such positions.[43]

In higher education, the unequal status of women as employees is demonstrated by patterns of pay inequity, denial of tenure and promotion, and other forms of discrimination. Substantial disparities exist in rank, tenure, and salary between male and female faculty members in colleges and universities. Over the last 30 years, the gap in salaries has actually increased[44] and the proportion of women granted tenure has shrunk[45] at some institutions.

Women, who make up about one-third of faculty members in colleges and universities, disproportionately occupy lower status positions as lecturers and instructors. While some women have been able to advance to assistant and associate professor positions, fewer have won promotions to the rank of full professor. While women make up 59 percent of instructors and 47 percent of assistant professors, they comprise only 35 percent of associate professors and 19 percent of full professors.[46] Women of color, even less well represented, account for fewer than 2 percent of full professors.[47]

Women's salaries are also considerably lower than men's salaries, even at the same rank. Female professors earn only 85 percent of the salaries of their male counterparts. The pay gap between male and female professors has actually grown 5 percent over the last 30 years. The average salary for a male full professor is $74,500; the average salary for a female at this level is $65,000. At the rank of instructor, the inequity persists. Men earn an average of $40,000; women, $35,000.[48] Women faculty are still less likely than men to earn tenure, become full professors, and achieve pay equity, and these problems are the most pervasive at the most prestigious colleges and universities.

A 1999 study at the Massachusetts Institute of Technology (MIT) revealed the entrenched, yet subtle, problem of sex discrimination against women. The study, conducted by a committee of women faculty in the School of Science, found that women faculty in the school received lower salaries and fewer research resources (including funding and laboratory space) and were excluded from important roles in their departments. The study also found that women faculty had more teaching and advising commitments, particularly with undergraduates.[49] Although MIT's women faculty received support from university administrators to remedy the documented problems, many more women faculty at colleges and universities across the country continue to face persistent discrimination in higher education.

Employee Protection From Sex Discrimination Under Title IX

Employees' protection from sex discrimination under Title IX is supported by the Supreme Court decision in *North Haven v. Bell* (1982)[50] and by two federal statutes, Title VII of the 1964 Civil Rights Act (prohibiting employment discrimination) and the 1963 Equal Pay Act. Although employees of educational institutions are covered under Title IX, OCR's authority is limited. OCR generally refers individual employee sex discrimination complaints to the Equal Employment Opportunity Commission, the federal administrative agency that investigates alleged violations of Title VII. OCR investigates only complaints that allege a pattern and practice of sex discrimination against a group of employees in an institution.

The regulations implementing Title IX at 34 C.F.R. Sections 106.51-106.61 protect employees in educational institutions against discrimination in the following areas:

Recruitment and Hiring

- Educational institutions cannot implement discriminatory policies and practices in the recruitment and hiring of employees.
- Institutions must administer nondiscriminatory practices in job advertising so that bias cannot exist in the classification of job qualifications.
- Institutions cannot discriminate during the application process through the use of employment criteria (such as a test) that have a disproportionately adverse effect on the basis of sex.
- Institutions cannot discriminate on the basis of marital or parental status in making employment decisions.
- Institutions must actively recruit applicants to overcome the effects of past or present discrimination in employment.

Promotion and Tenure

- Educational institutions cannot establish separate systems of promotion and tenure on the basis of sex.
- Institutions cannot establish separate policies on the basis of sex regarding job progression and job seniority.

Compensation and Benefits

- Educational institutions cannot establish policies that result in the payment of lower wages to employees on the basis of sex in jobs that require equal skill, effort, and responsibility if the jobs are performed under similar working conditions.
- Institutions cannot discriminate in the provision of benefits including medical insurance and retirement plans. Institutions must also provide leave for pregnancy and childbirth.

Complaints of Sex Discrimination Against Female Employees in Educational Institutions

Although employees in educational institutions accounted for only 9 percent of complainants in Title IX cases, our investigation revealed that these complaints cover important areas affected by sex discrimination in education. Among the most prevalent forms of sex discrimination are unfair practices in hiring and firing, promotion and tenure, and salary. Most complaints (29 of 36) were filed by female employees. Our analysis focuses on these cases.

Complaints of discrimination in hiring and firing represented 45 percent of cases filed by female employees in elementary and secondary schools and 27 percent of cases filed by female employees in colleges and universities. Complaints of discrimination in promotion and tenure accounted for 18 percent of cases filed by female employees in elementary and secondary schools and 27 percent of cases filed by female employees in colleges and universities.

Employees in educational institutions also face sexual harassment and retaliation. Complaints of sexual harassment by colleagues and administrators represented 18 percent of cases filed by female employees in elementary and secondary education and 63 percent of cases filed by female employees in higher education. Female faculty in colleges and universities also reported sexual harassment from male students in 9 percent of cases filed. Female employees in educational institutions also reported facing retaliation for engaging in a protected activity under Title IX such as filing a sexual harassment complaint. Retaliation complaints accounted for 64 percent of sex discrimination cases filed by female employees in elementary and secondary education and 27 percent of sex discrimination cases filed by female employees in higher education.

Case Studies: Sex Discrimination Against Female Employees in Educational Institutions

Although the Office for Civil Rights is limited in its authority to investigate complaints on behalf of employees, it investigated complaints that alleged a pattern and practice of sex discrimination against groups of female employees in schools and universities:

- Female representation in the top administrative ranks was investigated in the University of California statewide system of schools. The system's nine chancellors included only two women. In the history of the system, only four women have served as chancellor.

- Discrimination in the hiring of women as administrators was investigated in the Mora Public School system in New Mexico. OCR found that the system discriminated against women for principal, assistant superintendent, and superintendent positions.

- Promotion of women to full-time positions of professor, associate professor, and assistant professor in the Department of Social Sciences was investigated at Tarleton State University in Texas. OCR also investigated pay practices.

- Discrimination in the hiring of female physical education teachers was investigated in the Bamberg School District in South Carolina. The district's job announcement for a physical education teacher listed experience coaching football among the job qualifications.

OCR investigates discrimination in the hiring and promotion of women by reviewing the qualifications and requirements for the positions as stipulated by the educational institution. The agency then examines the applicant pool to determine whether women were considered at a rate comparable to their availability in the labor market. OCR negotiates a compliance agreement when there is evidence of a pattern of discrimination. The agreement seeks to remedy practices that deny opportunities to women employed in educational institutions. The agency may also require that the institutions employ practices to overcome the effects of past or present discrimination in employment.

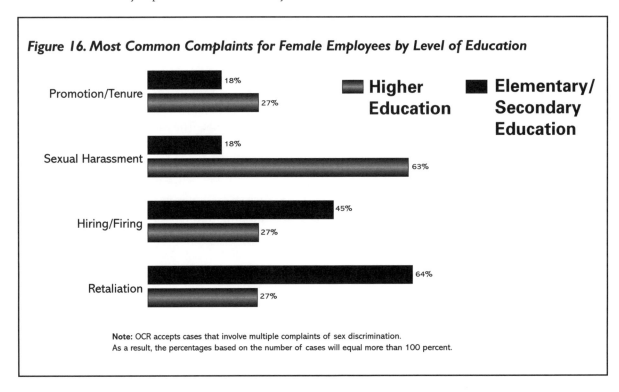

Figure 16. Most Common Complaints for Female Employees by Level of Education

Higher Education Elementary/Secondary Education

Promotion/Tenure — 18% / 27%

Sexual Harassment — 18% / 63%

Hiring/Firing — 45% / 27%

Retaliation — 64% / 27%

Note: OCR accepts cases that involve multiple complaints of sex discrimination.
As a result, the percentages based on the number of cases will equal more than 100 percent.

Chapter Three:
OCR Investigation of Title IX Complaints

The Office for Civil Rights regulates Title IX compliance through the investigation and resolution of complaints filed with the agency. To initiate an investigation of illegal sex discrimination, individuals must file a complaint with one of the 12 regional enforcement offices throughout the country. A complaint may be filed by anyone who believes that an institution covered by Title IX has discriminated against someone on the basis of sex. A person need not be a victim of the alleged discrimination to complain on behalf of another person or group facing sex discrimination. Organizations may also file complaints on behalf of victims of sex discrimination. Complaints may be filed on behalf of both male and female victims of sex discrimination.

Filing Procedures

Complaints must be filed within 180 days (six months) of the alleged discriminatory act; if the discrimination is ongoing, a complaint may be filed at any time. The complainant may want to become familiar with the grievance procedures of the institution against which the complaint has been filed, if the institution has such procedures as mandated by law. However, complainants are not required to use the institution's grievance procedure before filing a complaint with OCR. If the complainant chooses to file an internal grievance with the institution, he or she may re-file the complaint with the OCR within 60 days of the end of institution's investigation.

To file a formal complaint of sex discrimination, individuals must submit a letter to OCR. A discrimination complaint form is also available from the regional enforcement offices. The sex discrimination complaint should include the following information:

- The complainant's name, address, and (optional) telephone number. Even if the complainant would like to maintain confidentiality, the name of the complainant must be included in the complaint along with a request for anonymity.

- A general description of the class or party injured by the discrimination; however, the names of injured parties are not required.

- The name and address of the education institution committing the alleged acts of discrimination.

- A description of the alleged discriminatory acts with sufficient detail to facilitate a complete investigation. If the institution shows a pattern of discrimination, the complaint should describe all related incidents of discrimination. The complaint will be stronger if the complainant can demonstrate a general practice of discrimination rather than a single instance.

- The approximate dates of the discrimination and whether it is ongoing.

The complaint should also include names, addresses, and telephone numbers of others who may have additional information about the alleged discrimination. The complainant should indicate what information these individuals have to offer. The complainant has the right to request an interview by OCR during the investigation; however, OCR need not conduct such an interview without a formal request. If the complaint involves an emergency situation, the complainant may ask OCR to expedite the investigation. While OCR is not required to oblige, the knowledge of an impending serious injury may speed the agency's response.[1]

Issues and Problems with the Filing Process

By design, the process for filing a sex discrimination complaint is simple and straightforward, involving only the submission of a letter or form to the agency. Complainants do not need to seek legal counsel to file a complaint, thereby reducing the financial strain of fighting sex discrimination. To lessen the emotional strain, complainants can request confidentiality. However, several problems with the filing process limit opportunities to address sex discrimination in education.

To file a sex discrimination complaint, complainants must be aware of their rights under Title IX. Unfortunately, many institutions have not established grievance procedures to deal with sex discrimination complaints as required by law, and many more have not appointed a designated representative to address sex discrimination complaints as mandated. *As a result, complainants may not know what acts are considered illegal sex discrimination under Title IX.* Further, complainants may not know they have the option to pursue an OCR action against the institution. By failing to provide notice, these schools and universities deny complainants the opportunity to exercise their rights under Title IX.

The opportunity to exercise Title IX rights is further compounded by the six-month statute of limitations imposed by OCR on sex discrimination complaints. Although OCR will grant extensions in some instances, lack of knowledge about Title IX (or the agency) is not considered grounds for an extension. *These limitations deprive complainants who do not know about Title IX of the opportunity to exercise their rights under this statute.*

OCR's statute of limitations is not mandated by law; it is self-imposed. In the state and federal court system, the statute of limitations under Title IX is two to three years.[2] OCR should extend the statute of limitations for Title IX to match the courts.

Recommendations for Improving the Filing Process

Based on our review of sex discrimination complaints filed with OCR, we recommend that the agency take the following actions:

- Provide a checklist of possible areas of sex discrimination on a complaint form to ensure students and their parents have adequate knowledge about their rights under Title IX. The agency should continue to accept complaints submitted by letter with or without the complaint form.

- In *every complaint* of sex discrimination filed with the agency, determine whether the institution has complied with the notice provisions, designated an equity coordinator, and established grievance procedures. Such an investigation would confirm whether complainants knew about their Title IX rights.

- Initiate more compliance reviews to assess institutions' level of compliance with the Title IX requirements to appoint an equity coordinator and to establish grievance procedures.

- Extend the OCR-imposed statute of limitations for Title IX to match the two to three years allowed by the state and federal courts.

Case Studies: Filing a Timely Complaint Under the Statute of Limitations

A case in the Monroe County School District in Forsyth, Georgia, demonstrates how students' rights under Title IX are restricted by the statute of limitations imposed by the Office for Civil Rights. In 1994 the mother of a female student filed a complaint with OCR alleging that her daughter was harassed by a male student during the 1992-1993 school year. The school failed to stop the harassment against the student despite repeated complaints from her mother. The school had no policy for resolving complaints of sexual harassment.

Because the student's complaint of sexual harassment was untimely under the Title IX statute of limitations, OCR decided not to investigate. However, OCR ordered the school to develop policies and procedures on sex discrimination, including sexual harassment. The school agreed to disseminate the policies and procedures to teachers, students, and parents.

Although OCR negotiated an agreement with the school to adopt a sex discrimination policy, the agency did not adequately address the female student's problem and offered her no protection from sexual harassment. The student could not pursue an internal investigation because the school did not have a policy on sexual harassment. When OCR dismissed her complaint, it left the student without any means to pursue a remedy with her school.

We recommend that OCR investigate all complaints in which the institution is found to lack policies and procedures on sex discrimination.

Investigation Procedures

OCR receives about 500 sex discrimination complaints each year.[3] In addressing complaints, the agency follows established procedures.

Before opening an investigation, OCR must evaluate whether the complaint comes under its authority. OCR has jurisdiction only over complaints filed against institutions that receive federal financial assistance. The agency must also determine whether there are circumstances that limit its responsibility to investigate the complaint. For instance, OCR is not responsible for investigating complaints that come under the jurisdiction of another federal agency, complaints for which litigation has been filed with the courts, or complaints that are being investigated through the internal grievance procedures of an institution. OCR can also decide not to investigate complaints that are untimely or complaints that the agency deems completely without merit.[4]

OCR's decision to proceed initiates the information phase of the investigation. OCR's regional offices assume responsibility for this phase. A team of attorneys, investigators, and support staff gathers information about the allegations through documentation and interviews. The investigation team may request documentation from the educational institution and the complainant for review. Among the records subject to review by the investigation team are:

- the policies and procedures of the institution on sex discrimination
- the records of the institution's investigation (if the complainant filed an internal grievance prior to filing an OCR complaint)
- academic and employment records maintained by the institution regarding the issue under investigation
- information gathered through interviews with the institution's staff, faculty, and administrators[5]

The investigation team may also review any relevant information or documentation provided by the complainant. These materials might include contact information for witnesses to the incidents of discrimination. Interviews of these witnesses require the consent of the complainants and the witnesses. The written consent of parents or guardians is required for interviews of children under the age of 18. The collection of data through documentation and interviews concludes the information phase of the investigation.[6]

Next comes the analysis phase, in which the investigation team examines the information provided by the complainant and the recipient institution. Depending on the allegations in the complaint, the agency may employ general or specific standards of evidence to determine whether discrimination has occurred. For a general standard, the agency may compare the complainant to others who are similarly situated in the institution. The agency may also examine whether a legitimate nondiscriminatory explanation for the situation exists or whether such an explanation is merely a pretext for discrimination. The agency may also employ specific standards of evidence of discrimination based on the complaint allegations. The agency refers to the regulations and guidelines implementing Title IX to provide specific standards of evidence.

Once an investigation has ended, OCR prepares a report for the complainant and the institution. The report includes

- a statement of the complaint's allegations
- legal standards applicable to the allegations
- a statement of OCR's authority over the institution
- a summary and analysis of the information gathered by OCR during the investigation
- OCR's conclusions based on the evidence and the legal standards

If the investigation reveals evidence of discrimination by the institution, OCR proceeds to complaint resolution.[7]

Issues and Problems With Investigation Procedures

OCR's investigative role is critical to the enforcement of Title IX in educational institutions. Our examination revealed several problems that impede the agency's effective enforcement of Title IX.

Acceptance of Complaints for Investigation

During our four-year period of investigation, OCR denied investigation of more than half of the 2,000-plus sex discrimination complaints received. The complaints were most often denied on the basis of jurisdiction and statute of limitations. The inadequate proportion of sex discrimination complaints accepted for investigation impedes OCR's effective enforcement of Title IX.

Length of Investigation

Title IX enforcement is further impeded by the undue length of the investigations. OCR maintains only loose guidelines governing the time spent on investigating allegations. According to the complaint resolution manual, the agency is expected to complete the evaluation phase of the investigation within 30 days of receipt of the complaint. The manual also states that the complainant and the institution should receive contact from OCR every 60 days during the investigation. The agency is expected to develop a plan to complete investigations that have not been resolved within 180 days (six months) of receipt of the complaint. However, these general guidelines do not mandate that the agency complete the investigation within a specified time frame. Further, no accountability measures within the agency ensure the timely resolution of complaints.

Our examination of the investigation of sex discrimination complaints by OCR revealed the excessive length of the investigation process. The average investigation took more than 200 days, nearly seven months. Only about half of the complaint investigations were completed within 180 days (six months), and only three-quarters were completed within 270 days (nine months)—the length of a school year. Ten percent of complaint investigations were not completed after an entire year. Several complaint investigations took nearly three years (959 days for the longest investigation). Allowing investigations to drag out this long poses a hardship for complainants, particularly those who have already endured the lengthy process of filing an internal institutional complaint.

Our research also showed considerable differences in the length of complaint investigations by region. On average, only four regions completed investigations within six months. The other regions took an average of eight months. The two-month disparity may indicate that some offices are more effectively addressing issues of sex discrimination in schools and universities. The regions should report on effective practices and procedures used during complaint investigation to improve investigations. The disparity between regional offices impedes the effective enforcement of Title IX in educational institutions throughout the country.

Data Collection and Interview Methods

The means by which OCR collects data can hinder the investigation of sex discrimination. During an investigation, OCR may attempt to collect data that has been sorted by sex to compare the complainant's situation with that of similarly situated others. However, many schools and universities do not maintain academic and discipline records on the basis of sex. We found that when educational institutions do not make comparison data available to the agency, OCR cannot (and does not) make a determination of discrimination.

The agency also may try to collect and review the records of an educational institution's investigation into allegations of sex discrimination. However, many schools and universities do not have policies and procedures for investigating sex discrimination complaints filed by students and employees. And even those that do have such policies often fail to maintain any records of internal investigations.[8] As a result, many schools and universities avoid responsibility for providing evidence to the agency to resolve complaints of sex discrimination. By this dereliction of duty, they unfairly shift the burden of proof to the complainant.

Another concern with data collection is OCR's reliance on discretionary data in making its findings. While OCR does not require the complainant to file a grievance with the edu-

Figure 17: Length of Complaint Investigation (Average by Region)	
Regional Office	**Length of Complaint Investigation**
Region I Boston Office	202 days
Region II New York Office	225 days
Region III Philadelphia Office	246 days
Region IV Atlanta Office	177 days
Region V Chicago Office	161 days
Region VI Dallas Office	232 days
Region VII Kansas City Office	169 days
Region VIII Denver Office	196 days
Region IX San Francisco Office	191 days
Region X Seattle Office	274 days
Region XI* Washington DC Office	159 days
Region XV* Cleveland Office	271 days
Total average	206 days

* These regional offices investigated fewer than 10 cases during our investigation period, and as a result, these numbers may not be useful for comparison and analysis.

cational institution before registering a complaint with the agency, it relies on records from the institution's investigation to determine if a violation occurred. If the complainant does not use the grievance procedures of the institution (assuming these exist) it is unlikely that the agency will find the institution guilty of sex discrimination. The agency's dependence on institutional data to render its decisions compromises its integrity and conflicts with its mandate to investigate and resolve sex discrimination complaints on behalf of the complainant and independent of the institution.

The use of interviews to obtain information about alleged sex discrimination also raises concerns. The agency does not maintain guidelines on the nature or number of informants to be interviewed during an investigation. The agency may interview the complainant and the parents of the complainant as well as school faculty and administrators. Both the complainant and the institution may also refer other informants (such as witnesses to the acts of discrimination) for the agency to interview. In policy, OCR solicits information regarding the allegations of sex discrimination from both sides through such interviews. In practice, however, the agency sometimes relies more on interviews with faculty and administrators than on interviews with the complainant and the complainant's informants. As a result, the agency sometimes makes its determination not from the complainant's perspective, but from the perspective of the institution. The misuse of interviews during investigations can hinder the efforts of the agency to remedy sex discrimination for students and employees.

Case Study: Data Collection From Institutions

A case in Gainesville, Florida, illustrates how OCR's reliance on inadequate institutional data can hurt individuals who file complaints of sex discrimination.

The mother of a black male elementary school student in the Alachua County School District filed a complaint with OCR alleging that her son was punished more severely than white students and female students in his class. In its investigation, OCR found that the school did not maintain discipline records by race and sex. The agency could not make a determination of discrimination without information to compare the student's situation with that of other students at the school. Therefore, OCR determined that the evidence was insufficient to support a claim of a Title IX violation against the school. The decision allowed the school to avoid its responsibility to provide OCR adequate information for the resolution of complaints.

Case Study: Length of OCR Investigation

While the Office for Civil Rights imposes strict limits on the time it gives educational institutions to conduct internal complaint investigations, it is far more generous with itself. OCR's own investigations commonly exceed six months, thereby delaying or denying meaningful relief to complainants. A case in Sacramento, California, is an example.

A female trainee filed a complaint with OCR against the Truck Driving Academy in Sacramento. The trainee alleged in her complaint that she was sexually harassed by a male instructor and that the training academy had not resolved her complaint of sexual harassment after more than three months. OCR found that the Truck Driving Academy did not provide the trainee with a prompt and equitable resolution to her sexual harassment complaint. While the training academy's investigation exceeded three months (141 days), OCR's investigation into her complaint exceeded seven (218 days).

Recommendations for Improving the Investigation Process

We recommend that OCR take the following actions to improve the enforcement of Title IX through complaint investigation on behalf of students and employees:

- Establish measures (such as complaint forms) to outline the information needed from a complainant and improve the rate at which complaints are accepted for investigation.

- Reduce OCR investigation time to six months or less to better address sex discrimination in schools and universities.

- Work with Congress to mandate that institutions collect and sort data by sex pertaining to employment, academics, and discipline to facilitate the investigation of sex discrimination complaints.

- Establish measures to promote the uniform handling of complaint investigations from region to region. Require each region to report on effective practices and procedures for addressing issues of sex discrimination in complaint investigation. Identify the best practices and promote their uniform application.

- Designate specialists on issues of sex equity and discrimination in each regional office and in the national office to more effectively investigate complaints of sex discrimination.

Chapter Four:
Resolution and Monitoring of Complaints

The Office for Civil Rights may conclude an investigation of a sex discrimination complaint by proceeding to complaint resolution. The agency can enter into negotiations with the institution at any time during the investigation or at its completion to resolve the complaint. OCR may employ the following methods of complaint resolution:

- the facilitation of an agreement between the complainant and the institution

- the negotiation of an agreement with the institution resolving the complainant's allegations before completing an investigation

- the negotiation of an agreement with the institution based on the investigation results

- the determination of insufficient evidence to support a violation against the institution

- the initiation of formal enforcement through administrative proceedings to deny federal funds to the institution[1]

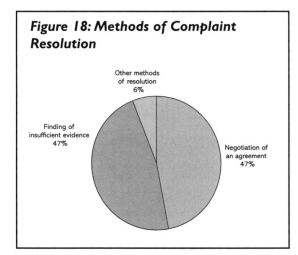

Figure 18: Methods of Complaint Resolution

Other methods of resolution 6%

Finding of insufficient evidence 47%

Negotiation of an agreement 47%

The negotiation of an agreement represents an effort by OCR to engage institutions in a voluntary resolution of the allegations in the sex discrimination complaint.

During discussions to resolve the complaint allegations, OCR negotiates the terms of an agreement with the institution to bring it into compliance with Title IX. The compliance agreement specifies the actions the institution will take to resolve the allegations in the complaint and the time frame in which it will take them. The compliance agreement also addresses any further institutional violations identified during the investigation (but not alleged by the complainant). The institution's remedial actions may include steps to identify and end the discrimination, as well as steps to remedy the discrimination's effects. By voluntarily signing the agreement with the agency, the institution avoids the risk of losing federal funding. An institution with violations is considered in compliance with Title IX once it accepts the terms of the compliance agreement.

OCR may consult with the complainant during the negotiation of the compliance agreement to ensure that the complainant's interests are addressed during resolution. If the complainant disagrees with the outcome of the investigation or the terms of the compliance agreement, he or she may convey these concerns to the regional office. On the basis of new information from the complainant, the agency may reconsider its findings or renegotiate the terms of the agreement. OCR also notifies the complainant that she or he may file a separate court action regardless of the agency's investigation and resolution of the complaint.

OCR monitors the institution's implementation of the compliance agreement. Schools must provide documentation of their actions to the agency at specified intervals. If the institution fails to implement the agreement within the designated time frame, the agency can renegotiate the terms of the agreement. Alternatively, the agency can initiate formal enforcement resulting in the termination of federal funds.

Issues and Problems With the Resolution and Monitoring Process

OCR's resolution and monitoring of sex discrimination complaints is crucial to the effective enforcement of Title IX in educational institutions. However, our examination of the facilitation of complaint resolution by the agency revealed problems that impede efforts to enforce Title IX.

Methods of Complaint Resolution

During the four-year period we investigated, most complaints of sex discrimination were resolved in one of two ways: through the negotiation of an agreement with the institution or through the determination of insufficient evidence to support a violation against the institution.

Complaints resolved through the facilitation of an agreement directly between the complainant and the institution were not included in our investigation because the agency does not monitor these complaints after resolution. During the period covered by our investigation, there were no complaints of sex discrimination resolved through the initiation of formal enforcement to deny federal funds to an institution. In fact, OCR has never exercised its authority to withhold federal funds from an offending institution for Title IX violations.

Our investigation revealed sex disparities in complaint resolution outcomes. More than half of the complaints filed by females were resolved by the negotiation of an agreement with the institution. In contrast, only about a third of cases filed by males resulted in a negotiated agreement. The remaining two-thirds (65 percent) of complaints filed by males were resolved through the determination of insufficient evidence. The high proportion of male complaints unsubstantiated by OCR investigation may indicate that the agency should redirect the resources allocated for complaint resolution in this area. Through the use of compliance reviews, the agency might more effectively investigate reports of sex discrimination against males in educational institutions.

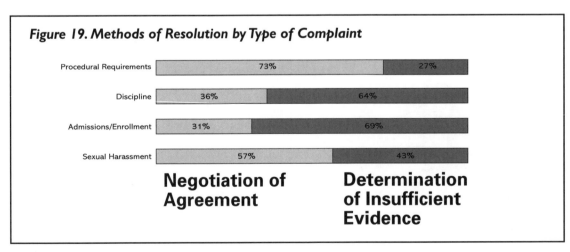

Figure 19. Methods of Resolution by Type of Complaint

	Negotiation of Agreement	Determination of Insufficient Evidence
Procedural Requirements	73%	27%
Discipline	36%	64%
Admissions/Enrollment	31%	69%
Sexual Harassment	57%	43%

Figure 20. Methods of Complaint Resolution by Region		
Regional Office	**Negotiation of an Agreement**	**Determination of Insufficient Evidence**
Region I Boston Office	60%	37%
Region II New York Office	44%	56%
Region III Philadelphia Office	64%	36%
Region IV Atlanta Office	33%	67%
Region V Chicago Office	11%	89%
Region VI Dallas Office	37%	59%
Region VII Kansas City Office	61%	36%
Region VIII Denver Office	72%	28%
Region IX San Francisco Office	49%	46%
Region X Seattle Office	31%	66%
Region XI* Washington DC Office	50%	50%
Region XV* Cleveland Office	100%	0%
Average	**47%**	**47%**

These regional offices investigated fewer than 10 cases during our investigation period, and as a result, these numbers may not be useful for comparison and analysis.

Case resolution also varies by complaint type. Sexual harassment complaints—most of them filed by female students—were usually resolved through the negotiation of a compliance agreement. Complaints of discrimination in admissions and discipline—most of them filed by male students—were usually found to lack sufficient evidence. Complaints of nonadherence to procedural requirements (failing to appoint an equity coordinator and establish grievance procedures) were generally resolved through negotiations with the institution. These latter complaints were most often filed in connection with sexual harassment complaints; even when the harassment could not be substantiated through an agency investigation, procedural complaints often resulted in the negotiation of a compliance agreement.

This outcome suggests that the agency should evaluate school grievance policies and procedures with each investigation to more effectively enforce Title IX. Given that most admissions and discipline cases are found lacking in evidence, OCR should initiate more compliance reviews to assess whether discipline and admissions policies and procedures are implemented equitably. The agency should also initiate more compliance reviews to assess whether institutions are in compliance with the procedural requirements under Title IX.

Our investigation also revealed disparities between the regions in complaint resolution outcomes. Only four regions resolved complaints through the negotiation of a compliance agreement in more than 60 percent of cases. In two regions, more than 60 percent of cases were resolved through the determination of insufficient evidence. In another region, nearly 90 percent of cases were considered to have insufficient evidence to support a Title IX violation. The high proportion of cases found lacking in sufficient evidence severely limits the effective enforcement of Title IX by the agency.

Based on our investigation, compliance reviews are more effective than complaint resolution in addressing sex discrimination. OCR found violations requiring corrective action in two-thirds of compliance reviews but in less than one-half of complaints filed with the agency. Compliance reviews were also more effective in negotiating a compliance agreement. The period for monitoring the compliance agreement was longer—five years, as compared to a maximum of two years for monitoring agreements after complaint resolution.

Compliance Agreements

The exceedingly liberal nature of the compliance agreement negotiated between OCR and an educational institution can impede effective Title IX enforcement. Under the terms of the usual agreement, OCR equates compliance with a school's acceptance (not implementation) of contract provisions. In other words, a school with an uncorrected Title IX violation is considered fully compliant with the law as soon as it agrees to a specified remedy but before it takes any action.[2]

OCR's premature designation of compliance removes the impetus for an institution to remedy sex discrimination. The agency should adopt a new designation—conditional compliance—for institutions that have agreed to remedy discrimination but have not yet completed the terms of a compliance agreement. The agency should also reconsider the use of voluntary compliance agreements as the only penalty for violations.

Inconsistencies in the provisions of compliance agreements implemented by the various regional offices create further problems. OCR does not maintain guidelines on appropriate measures to remedy problems of sex discrimination in educational institutions. As a result, the regional offices often propose disparate solutions for similar problems and allot disparate time frames for monitoring compliance. Most regional offices monitor compliance for six months to one year. However, in some cases, the regional office monitors the agreement for three months or less. Only a few regional offices monitor an institution for compliance for more than a year, or sometimes two years. These disparities between regional offices threaten the effective enforcement of Title IX throughout the country.

OCR should require regional offices to report on the remedies used to address various types of institutional violations. The agency should then use this information to develop matrices of actions to be required of institutions, according to the type of violation addressed by the com-

Figure 21. Institute With Repeat Offenses of Sex Discrimination (1993-1997)	
Institution	Number of Offenses
Aiken County School District Aiken, SC	3
Arizona State University Tempe, AZ	2
California State University Fresno, CA	2
Campbell Union School District San Jose, CA	2
Central Washington University Ellensberg, WA	2
Columbia University New York, NY	2
D-Q University Davis, CA	3
Fairbanks School District Fairbanks, AK	2
Florida State University Tallahassee, FL	2
Humboldt State University Arcata, CA	2
Kent State University Kent, OH	2
Leavenworth Unified School District Leavenworth, KS	2
Orange Unified School District Orange, CA	2
Prince Georges County School Upper Marlboro, MD	3
Rhinebeck Central School District Rhinebeck, NY	2
State University of New York Buffalo, NY	2
Tacoma School District Tacoma, WA	2
University of Arizona Tuscon, AZ	2
University of Chicago Chicago, IL	3
University of Hawaii – Manoa Honolulu, HI	2
University of Maryland College Park, MD	2
University of Massachusetts Amherst, MA	2
University of North Carolina Chapel Hill, NC	2
Virginia Commonwealth University Richmond, VA	2

pliance agreement. OCR should also determine standards for monitoring compliance agreements by regional offices.

Repeat Offenders: Institutions With Multiple Complaints of Sex Discrimination

Our research revealed that roughly two dozen educational institutions—a disturbing 15 percent of the pool—were under investigation by the Office for Civil Rights for multiple cases of sex discrimination. In nearly 67 percent of these cases, the institutions were under investigation for repeat offenses.

Repeat offenders were not dealt with strictly enough by the agency; sometimes OCR allowed them to sign another compliance agreement to address the same violations as previous agreements. We recommend that the agency enforce the law more vigorously by eliminating federal funding for institutions with repeat violations within a specified time frame. OCR undermines its own authority by allowing institutions to commit repeat violations against Title IX.

Case Studies: Repeat Offenders

During the period covered by our investigation, the Office for Civil Rights investigated a considerable number of institutions for repeated violations of Title IX—often involving the same type of complaint. OCR often mishandled complaints against these institutions and thus failed to prevent repeat occurrences of discrimination. Three separate cases filed over three years in Arcata, California, demonstrate the problem.

In each case, OCR found that Humboldt State University failed to adequately and promptly investigate complaints of sexual harassment because of deficiencies in its grievance procedures. And in each case, OCR gave the university the opportunity to enter into a voluntary agreement to remedy the deficiencies identified. The persistence of the same grievance procedure deficiencies after three years—and repeated negotiations—casts doubt on the sincerity of the university's efforts to eliminate sex discrimination. OCR should have moved to withhold federal funds from Humboldt State University. By allowing Humboldt State to commit repeat violations without penalty, the agency undermined its own authority to enforce Title IX.

Recommendations for Improving the Resolution and Monitoring Process

Based on our investigation of the resolution and monitoring of complaints of sex discrimination by the Office for Civil Rights, we make the following recommendations to improve OCR's enforcement of Title IX:

- Establish measures to increase the proportion of complaints that proceed to compliance agreement negotiations during complaint resolution.

- Designate institutions with outstanding violations to be in conditional compliance pending implementation of the compliance agreement. Pursue harsher penalties for institutions that do not fully implement the agreements and for institutions with repeat violations.

- Develop guidelines for actions to be required of institutions by the regional offices according to the type of violations addressed in the compliance agreement. Establish time frames for monitoring compliance agreements by the regional offices.

- Increase the use of compliance reviews as a more effective means of addressing sex discrimination in educational institutions.

Chapter Five:
Action Agenda for Title IX

The purpose of the AAUW Legal Advocacy Fund report on Title IX is to recognize OCR's progress in implementing Title IX and to call attention to the problems that impede its effective enforcement. Our report seeks to further the progress toward the elimination of sex discrimination in education through Title IX enforcement. We offer the following action agenda to help accelerate the equity advancements made possible by Title IX to ensure an equitable education for all students in our schools and universities.

Agenda for Congress

Title IX enforcement depends on support from federal and state legislation. Title IX also depends on support from court decisions at the state and federal levels. Our examination of the legal status of Title IX reveals substantial threats to the efforts to effectively enforce the legislation. Since the passage of Title IX in 1972, the legislation has been threatened by Supreme Court rulings that sought to narrow its scope and by acts of Congress to eliminate funding for enforcement. To bolster the legislation against such attacks, we recommend our action agenda for Congress.

Funding for the Office for Civil Rights

Congress must increase funding for OCR, the primary agency responsible for the enforcement of civil rights legislation in educational institutions. At present, Congress allocates very limited funding given OCR's broad responsibility for countering discrimination in schools and universities. The agency supports an overwhelming caseload (more than 5,000 complaints every year) in its efforts to monitor compliance with the federal statutes that prohibit discrimination in educational institutions receiving federal financial assistance. In 1998 Congress appropriated only $60 million for OCR—less than $1 for each student in our nation's schools and universities.[1] Such underfunding severely limits the actions the agency can initiate to address sex discrimination in education. Most of OCR's resources are spent to resolve complaints filed with the agency (90 percent of agency funding was spent on case resolution in 1993).[2] Thus, the agency has only limited resources available for compliance reviews and technical assistance. Our report found agency-initiated action such as compliance reviews to be more effective than complaint resolution in addressing sex discrimination, yet—because of demand—the agency spends nearly all its resources on complaint resolution.

Continued Funding for Title IX

Congress must continue to support Title IX through funding for the Women's Educational Equity Act (WEEA) and for Title IV of the 1964 Civil Rights Act. Congress must also take action to increase the funding for both programs to advance the efforts to eliminate sex discrimination in education. Funding for these programs is extremely limited: In 1999 Congress allocated only $500,000 for the WEEA Equity Resource Center—down from nearly $6 million in 1974—and even this scant sum was nearly eliminated by the 1999 reauthorization of the Elementary and Secondary Education Act. WEEA has never been adequately funded by

Congress. After its best year in 1974, funding for WEEA diminished steadily throughout the 1980s, at a rate of almost $1 million a year, until reaching current levels.[3] This report shows that while efforts to eliminate sex discrimination in education have met with some success, the progress has not been sufficient to eliminate the only federally funded program dedicated to promoting gender equity in education.

Supplemental Funding for Title IX

Congress should also provide federal funding to educational institutions and state education agencies to improve the enforcement of Title IX; the funding should particularly target the support of Title IX coordinators. Although Title IX requires each federally funded educational institution to appoint an individual to coordinate activities in response to the law, Title IX does not specify those activities to be conducted, nor does it authorize funds to support this position. Because of funding shortages, fewer than 25 states have a Title IX coordinator.[4] Congress has provided funding—since eliminated—to support sex equity coordinators under vocational education legislation such as the Carl Perkins Act of 1984. Such funding can and should be restored and provided to educational institutions under Title IX.

Agenda for the Office for Civil Rights

OCR's role in investigating and resolving sex discrimination complaints is particularly critical given that most schools and universities do not have policies and procedures to address these as mandated by law under Title IX. To improve OCR's efforts to enforce Title IX, we recommend the following action agenda:

Complaint Investigation and Resolution

OCR should consider the problems identified in our report to improve the investigation and resolution of sex discrimination complaints.

- To encourage the filing of actionable complaints, OCR should extend the statute of limitations on Title IX and develop a standard complaint form with a checklist of alleged Title IX violations.

- To promote the investigation of complaints by the agency, OCR should develop measures to ensure that a greater proportion of complaints is accepted for investigation by the agency.

- The agency should complete investigations of complaints within six months.

- The resolution and monitoring of complaints by the agency could be improved by developing guidelines for the negotiation of compliance agreements and time frames for monitoring these agreements.

- The national office should coordinate regional office efforts to implement reforms in the investigation and resolution of complaints by requiring each regional office to report on effective practices and procedures for addressing issues of sex discrimination.

- OCR should also designate equity specialists in sex discrimination issues in the national and regional offices to improve the effective enforcement of Title IX.

Compliance Reviews

OCR should increase the number of compliance reviews focused on sex discrimination so that the percentage of compliance reviews is at least proportionate to the percentage of sex discrimination complaints filed with the agency each year. OCR should also consider the use of compliance reviews as a means of more effectively enforcing Title IX in educational institutions. Our research demonstrated that compliance reviews are a more effective means for addressing sex discrimination than complaint resolution. The use of compliance reviews was also more effective in negotiating a compliance agreement with the institution.

Policy Guidance

The Office for Civil Rights should issue policy guidance to direct the efforts of educational institutions to deal with areas of sex discrimination in which there has been little guidance by the agency, the legislature, and the courts. Given our evidence on widespread institutional noncompliance with procedural requirements, the agency should develop guidelines for educational institutions on the appointment of a sex equity coordinator and the development of grievance procedures. OCR should further identify the specific activities to be conducted by the sex equity coordinators. The agency should also continue efforts to revise guidelines on sexual harassment following recent court decisions affecting the liability of educational institutions in this area. OCR may also need to clarify regulations regarding school discipline and the use of standardized tests in admissions—both of which have been identified as prevalent areas of sex discrimination in schools and universities.

Sanctioning Institutions for Violations

Given that educational institutions have been subject to the mandate of Title IX for almost 30 years, OCR should begin to pursue harsher penalties for schools that do not fully implement compliance agreements, and for schools with multiple offenses of sex discrimination. The agency should also designate institutions with violations to be in conditional compliance during the implementation of the compliance agreement; institutions should be considered in compliance only upon completion of the terms of the compliance agreement.

Data Collection on Sex Discrimination in Educational Institutions

OCR should work with Congress to mandate that schools and universities collect and separate employment, academic, and discipline records by sex and race to facilitate the investigation and resolution of sex discrimination complaints. The agency should also work with Congress to mandate that institutions submit compliance reports on a regular basis as a condition of receiving federal funds. Title IX regulations required an initial evaluation of compliance to be conducted by institutions. However, the results of these evaluations were not collected or monitored by OCR. Given the evidence of continued sex discrimination in all areas of education, the agency must require institutions to re-evaluate their compliance status regularly.

Collaboration Among Government Agencies

The Office for Civil Rights should continue recent efforts to coordinate an interagency enforcement initiative to increase efforts to enforce Title IX in educational institutions.[5] Any federal agency that provides funds for educational programs and activities is authorized to enforce Title IX. Each federal agency should develop plans for enforcing Title IX, including regulations and procedures for handling complaints of sex discrimination.

Agenda for Schools and Universities

To ensure an equitable education for all students in our nation's schools and universities, Title IX compliance must become a priority of educational institutions. OCR, with its limited budget and overwhelming caseload, can't see to the enforcement alone. While OCR investigates sex discrimination in about 500 schools and universities each year, it cannot apply the same level of scrutiny to the more than 15,000 school districts and almost 4,000 colleges and universities across the country. We offer our agenda to our nation's institutions that must take action to address the problem of sex discrimination in education.

Compliance With Procedural Requirements Under Title IX

Schools and universities must comply with Title IX procedural requirements. Our research revealed that most institutions fail to establish grievance procedures, appoint a designated representative, and publish public notices of nondiscrimination as mandated by law under Title IX. Previous research has demonstrated that schools and universities without grievance procedures are considerably less likely to take action against sex discrimination.[6] Schools and universities must adopt and publish grievance procedures on sex discrimination for students and employees and develop and implement procedures for investigating and resolving complaints of sex discrimination. Schools and universities must also appoint and support an equity coordinator to monitor compliance by the institution with Title IX.

Data Collection and Compliance Reports

Schools and universities must collect and separate employment, academic, and discipline records by sex to facilitate the investigation and resolution of sex discrimination complaints by the institution and by outside agencies. Institutions should also maintain records of investigations of complaints of sex discrimination. Institutions should conduct annual compliance surveys to assess the problem of sex discrimination. The results of these surveys should be submitted to OCR on a regular basis as a condition of receiving federal funds.

Training for Faculty, Staff, and Students

Schools and universities need to conduct training for faculty, staff, and students to remedy and prevent sex discrimination violations in education. Our research found that schools and universities with Title IX violations are often required to provide such training as a condition of the compliance agreement. Institutions can provide faculty and staff with in-service training sessions addressing sex discrimination for professional development credit. Institutions can also make materials and training available for faculty and staff to incorporate anti-bias content and pedagogy into the curriculum for students. Through these activities, schools and universities can fulfill their obligation to inform students and employees of their rights under Title IX.

Partnerships With Parents and Community

Schools and universities should also forge community partnerships with law enforcement agencies, interest groups, and parents in an effort to eliminate sex discrimination in education.

Appendix A
National and Regional Offices of the Office for Civil Rights

National Office

U.S. Department of Education
Office for Civil Rights
Mary E. Switzer Bldg.
330 C St. SW
Washington, DC 20202
Phone: (800) 421-3481
Fax: (202) 205-9862
TDD: (202) 205-5166
Email: OCR@ed.Gov
Homepage:
http://www.ed.gov/offices/OCR/

Eastern Division

Connecticut, Maine, Massachusetts, New Hampshire, Rhode Island, Vermont
Office for Civil Rights, Boston Office
U.S. Department of Education
J. W. McCormack Post Office & Courthouse, Rm. 707
Boston, MA 02109-4557
Phone: (617) 223-9662
Fax: (617) 223-9669
TDD: (617) 223-9695
Email: OCR_Boston@ed.gov

New Jersey, New York, Puerto Rico, Virgin Islands
Office for Civil Rights, New York Office
U. S. Department of Education
75 Park Pl. 14th Floor
New York, NY 10007-2146
Phone: (212) 637-6466
Fax: (212) 264-3803
TDD: (212) 637-0478
Email: OCR_NewYork@ed.gov

Delaware, Maryland, Kentucky, Pennsylvania, West Virginia
Office for Civil Rights, Philadelphia Office
U.S. Department of Education
Wanamaker Bldg., Ste. 515
100 Penn Square East
Philadelphia, PA 19107
Phone: (215) 656-8541
Fax: (215) 656-8605
TDD: (215) 656-8604
Email: OCR_Philadelphia@ed.gov

Southern Division

Alabama, Florida, Georgia, South Carolina, Tennessee
Office for Civil Rights, Atlanta Office
U.S. Department of Education
61 Forsyth St. SW
Atlanta, GA 30303-3104
Phone: (404) 562-6350
Fax: (404) 562-6455
TDD: (404) 331-7236
Email: OCR_Atlanta@ed.gov

Arkansas, Louisiana, Mississippi, Oklahoma, Texas
Office for Civil Rights, Dallas Office
U.S. Department of Education
1999 Bryan St. Ste. 2600
Dallas, TX 75201
Phone: (214) 880-2459
Fax: (214) 880-3082
TDD: (214) 880-2456
Email: OCR_Dallas@ed.gov

North Carolina, Virginia, Washington, DC

Office for Civil Rights, DC Office
U.S. Department of Education
1100 Pennsylvania Ave. NW, Rm. 316
P.O. Box 14620
Washington, DC 20044-4620
Phone: (202) 208-2545
Fax: (202)-208-7797
TDD: (202) 208-7741
Email: OCR_DC@ed.gov

Midwestern Division

Illinois, Indiana, Minnesota, Wisconsin

Office for Civil Rights, Chicago Office
U.S. Department of Education
111 N. Canal St. Ste. 1053
Chicago, IL 60606-7204
Phone: (312) 886-8434
Fax: (312) 353-4888
TDD: (312) 353-2540
Email: OCR_Chicago@ed.gov

Michigan and Ohio

Office for Civil Rights, Cleveland Office
U.S. Department of Education
600 Superior Ave. East
Bank One Ctr. Rm. 750
Cleveland, OH 44114-2611
Phone: (216) 522-4970
Fax: (216) 522-2573
TDD: (216) 522-4944
Email: OCR_Cleveland@ed.gov

Iowa, Kansas, Missouri, Nebraska, North Dakota, South Dakota

Office for Civil Rights, Kansas City Office
U.S. Department of Education
10220 N. Executive Hills Blvd. 8th Floor
Kansas City, MO 64153-1367
Phone: (816) 880-4200
Fax: (816) 891-0644
TDD: (816) 891-0582
Email: OCR_KansasCity@ed.gov

Western Division

Arizona, Colorado, Montana, New Mexico, Utah, Wyoming

Office for Civil Rights, Denver Office
U.S. Department of Education
Federal Bldg. Ste. 310
1244 Speer Boulevard
Denver, CO 80204-3582
Phone: (303) 844-5695
Fax: (303) 844-4303
TDD: (303) 844-3417
Email: OCR_Denver@ed.gov

California

Office for Civil Rights, San Francisco Office
U.S. Department of Education
Old Federal Bldg.
50 United Nations Plaza, Rm. 239
San Francisco, CA 94102-4102
Phone: (415) 556-4275
Fax: (415) 437-7786
TDD: (415) 437-7783
Email: OCR_SanFrancisco@ed.gov

Alaska, Hawaii, Idaho, Nevada, Oregon, Washington, American Samoa, Guam, Pacific Islands

Office for Civil Rights, Seattle Office
U.S. Department of Education
915 Second Ave. Rm. 3310
Seattle, WA 98174-1099
Phone: (206) 220-7900
Fax: (206) 220-7887
TDD: (206) 220-7907
Email: OCR_Seattle@ed.gov

Appendix B
Internet Resources on Title IX

Education Resources

American School Board Journal
http://www.asbj.com
Offers practical advice on a broad range of topics pertinent to school governance and management, policy-making, student achievement, and school leadership. Covers education news, school law, research, and new books.

Education Week
http://www.edweek.com
Covers local, state, and national news and issues from preschool through the 12th grade. Provides special reports on issues such as sexual harassment in schools.

National Center for Education Statistics (NCES)
http://nces.ed.gov
The primary federal agency responsible for the collection, analysis, and reporting of data related to education in the United States. NCES maintains data relevant to equity issues in education.

Office for Civil Rights
http://www.ed.gov/offices/OCR/
The agency within the Department of Education that regulates and enforces civil rights laws against discrimination in programs and activities receiving federal financial assistance.

United States Department of Education
http://www.ed.gov
The cabinet-level department responsible for national efforts to improve education at all levels through financial and programmatic support.

Women's Educational Equity Act (WEEA) Resource Center
http://www.edc.org/WomensEquity/
The U.S. Department of Education program dedicated to reducing the educational disparity between males and females .The WEEA Resource Center works with schools, community organizations, businesses, and individuals to publish and market gender-fair education products; fight against discrimination based on gender, race, class, language, and disability; and disseminate resources for multicultural gender-fair education.

Legal Resources

FedLaw
http://fedlaw.gsa.gov
Provides access to legal resources and information including civil rights and equal opportunity legislation.

Legal Information Institute - Supreme Court Decisions
http://supct.law.cornell.edu/supct/
Offers U.S. Supreme Court opinions issued since May 1990.

United States Congress on the Internet
http://thomas.loc.gov/home/thomas2.html
A searchable database about past and current legislation in Congress, provided by the Library of Congress.

Organizations

Alliance for Justice
http://www.afj.org
A national association of environmental, civil rights, mental health, women's, children's and consumer advocacy organizations.

American Association of University Women (AAUW)

http://www.aauw.org

A national nonprofit organization that promotes education and equity for all women and girls. AAUW comprises three corporations: the member Association, the Educational Foundation, and the Legal Advocacy Fund.

AAUW Educational Foundation

http://www.aauw.org/7000/aboutef.html

The largest source of funding exclusively for graduate women in the United States and abroad. The Foundation also commissions pivotal research on women and education.

AAUW Legal Advocacy Fund

http://www.aauw.org/7000/aboutlaf.html

The nation's largest legal fund focused solely on sex discrimination in higher education. It provides funding and support for women seeking judicial redress for sex discrimination.

American Civil Liberties Union (ACLU)

http://www.aclu.org

An organization that advocates for individual rights by litigating, legislating, and educating the public on a broad array of issues affecting individual freedom in the United States. ACLU operates searchable databases of issues relating to students' rights and women's rights.

Citizens' Commission on Civil Rights

http://www.cccr.org

Nonprofit group committed to the revitalization of a progressive civil rights agenda at the national level to fight bias and discrimination; promote equality of opportunity in education, employment, and housing; further political and economic empowerment; and guarantee equal treatment in the administration of justice. Promotes civil rights enforcement as a duty and obligation of the federal government.

Feminist Majority Foundation

http://www.feminist.org

An organization committed to achieving political, economic, and social equality for women. It provides information about current legislation concerning equity issues in education.

National Organization for Women (NOW)

http://www.now.org

A feminist organization committed to promoting equity for women. NOW provides legislative updates and action alerts on issues related to equity in education.

National Organization for Women Legal Defense and Education Fund (NOW LDEF)

http://www.nowldef.org

Pursues equality for women and girls in the workplace, schools, family, and courts through litigation, education, and public information.

National Women's Law Center

http://www.nwlc.org

Litigates and advocates for women's legal rights in employment, child and adult dependent care, reproductive rights, child support enforcement, educational opportunity, and Social Security.

Security on Campus Inc.

http://www.soconline.org

A nonprofit organization geared to preventing campus violence and crimes and assisting campus victims in the enforcement of their legal rights.

Women's Sports Foundation

http://www.womenssportsfoundation.org/templates/

A national nonprofit, member-based organization dedicated to increasing opportunities for girls and women in sports and fitness through education, advocacy, recognition, and grants.

Publications on the Internet

American Association of University Women Educational Foundation

The AAUW Report: How Schools Shortchange Girls (1992)

http://www.aauw.org/2000/research.html

Hostile Hallways: The AAUW Report on Sexual Harassment in America's Schools (1993)

http://www.aauw.org/2000/research.html

Separated by Sex: A Critical Look at Single-Sex Education for Girls (1998)
http://www.aauw.org/2000/research.html

Gender Gaps: Where Schools Still Fail Our Children (1998)
http://www.aauw.org/2000/research.html

Gaining a Foothold: Women's Transitions Through Work and College (1999)
http://www.aauw.org/2000/research.html

Voices of a Generation: Teenage Girls on Sex, School, and Self (1999)
http://www.aauw.org/2000/research.html

Tech-Savvy: Educating Girls in the New Computer Age (2000)
http://www.aauw.org/2000/research.html

Citizens' Commission on Civil Rights

The Test of Our Progress: The Clinton Record on Civil Rights (1999)
http://www.cccr.org/ccrreport13.html

Education Week

A Trust Betrayed: Sexual Abuse by Teachers (1998)
http://www.edweek.com/sreports/abuse98.htm

National Organization for Women Legal Defense and Education Fund

An Annotated Summary of the Regulations for Title IX
http://www.nowldef.org/html/issues/edu/publicat.htm

Legal Resource Kit: Sexual Harassment in the Schools
http://www.nowldef.org/html/pub/kits.htm

Secrets in Public: Sexual Harassment in Our Schools
http://www.nowldef.org/html/issues/edu/publicat.htm

Office for Civil Rights

Protecting Students From Harassment and Hate Crime: A Guide for Schools (1999)
http://www.ed.gov/pubs/Harassment/

Sexual Harassment Guidance: Harassment of Students by School Employees, Other Students, or Third Parties
http://www.ed.gov/offices/OCR/sexhar01.html

U.S. Department of Education

Title IX, Education Amendments of 1972
http://www.dol.gov/dol/oasam/public/regs/statutes/titleix.htm

Title IX: 25 Years of Progress (1997)
http://www.ed.gov/pubs/TitleIX/

Women's Educational Equity Act Resource Center

Facts on Title IX: Before and After
http://www.edc.org/WomensEquity/title9/digest/digest.htm

Raising the Grade: A Title IX Curriculum
http://www.edc.org/womensequity/resource/title9/raising/index.htm

Title IX: A Brief History
http://www.edc.org/womensequity/resource/title9/digest/digest.htm

Title IX and Sexual Harassment
http://www.edc.org/womensequity/resource/title9/digest/harass.htm

Title IX at 25: A Report Card on Gender Equity
http://www.edc.org/womensequity/resource/title9/report/index.htm

Title IX: Before and After
http://www.edc.org/womensequity/resource/title9/before.htm

Women's Sports Foundation

Research Reports
http://www.womenssportfoundation.org/templates/store/index.html#8

About the Researchers

Jennifer L. Engle is a doctoral fellow in education at the American University in Washington, D.C. Her research interests focus on issues of equity and access in education, and her program of study is concentrated in educational equity and policy. She works as a research assistant with David Sadker, an expert in gender equity in education. She has a bachelor's degree in women's studies and psychology and a master's degree in education.

Paula Zimmerman graduated from George Washington University law school in May 2000. She had just completed her first year of law school when she joined LAF as a summer intern to conduct Title IX research. Paula received a bachelor of arts degree in political science from Bucknell University in 1997.

Beth Hoffman is a senior litigation attorney who practiced law in New York for more than 25 years. As an attorney and partner with the law firm Bouvier, O'Connor for more than 20 years, she specialized in family law and general business and estate law in addition to her civil trial work. She recently moved to Arizona and was admitted to the Arizona State Bar.

Selected List of Reviewers and Advisers

Lynn Fox is an associate professor in the School of Education at American University in Washington, D.C., where she teaches courses in educational psychology, educational assessment, and research methods. She received her doctorate in educational psychology from Johns Hopkins University, where she served as co-director of the Study of Mathematically Precocious Youth between 1971-1974 and coordinator of the Intellectually Gifted Child Study Group. She is the chair of the Math, Science and Technology subpanel of the Gender Equity Expert Panel for the U.S. Department of Education. Her book, *The Gender Equity Expert Panel: Visions and Realities; A History of the Gender Equity Expert Panel* (Washington, D.C., Government Printing Office) is forthcoming. Among her numerous other publications credits, she is the co-author, with Andrea I. Prejean, of *Bright Child: A Guide for Parents and Teachers of Young Gifted Children* (Manassas, Va.: Gifted Education Press, 1999) and editor, with Linda Brody and Dianne Tobin, of *Learning-Disabled/Gifted Children: Identification and Programming* (Baltimore: University Park Press, 1983).

Phyllis Lerner is director of Interweave, a Bethesda, Maryland, organization specializing in educational equity and effectiveness training. Interweave programs, typically designed for teachers and administrators from preschool through graduate school, have also been adapted for community groups, including parents, social service personnel, and business leaders. Lerner has nearly three decades of experience in teaching at the elementary, secondary, and university levels. She has served as a special service consultant for the California State Department of Education. She assisted in the development of and appeared in a Master of Arts in Teaching video series produced and disseminated by Lee Canter Educational Productions. She also worked to produce, direct, and present a gender equity in-service series for the Educational Channel and Baltimore County Public Schools. She took part in similar programs with Public Broadcasting in Massachusetts and Virginia.

As a national gender equity trainer and a leader in issues ranging from effectiveness in teaching to equity in athletics, Lerner has appeared on a variety of local and national public radio and television shows, and has been an invited speaker at hundreds of conferences.

David Sadker, a professor in the School of Education at American University in Washington, D.C., has taken part in training programs to combat sexism and sexual harassment in more than 40 states and overseas. He has directed more than a dozen federal equity grants and authored five books and more than 75 articles in journals such as *Phi Delta Kappan, Harvard Educational Review,* and *Psychology Today*. His research and writing document sex bias from the classroom to the boardroom. He has published and trained in areas ranging from bias in professional communications to sexual harassment, and teaches effective strategies in management as well as the classroom.

Sadker's work with his late wife Myra has been reported in hundreds of newspapers and magazines including *USA Today, USA Weekend, Parade Magazine, Business Week, The Washington Post, The London Times, The New York Times, Time,* and *Newsweek*. The Sadkers appeared on local and national television and radio shows such as The Today Show, Good Morning America, The Oprah Winfrey Show, Phil Donahue's The Human Animal, National Public Radio's All Things Considered and twice on Dateline: NBC with Jane Pauley. In 1991 David Sadker received the American Educational Research Association's award for the best review of research published in the United States. He also won the association's professional service award in 1995 and the Eleanor Roosevelt Award from the American Association of University Women Educational Foundation in 1995. David and Myra Sadkers' book, *Failing at Fairness: How Our Schools Cheat Girls*, was published by Touchstone Press in 1995.

Endnotes

Executive Summary

1 U.S. Department of Education, Office for Civil Rights, *Annual Report to Congress: Fiscal Year 1997* (Washington, D.C., 1997).

Introduction

1 *Summary of the Regulations for Title IX of the Education Amendments of 1972* (New York: NOW Legal Defense and Education Fund, 1997).

2 *Ibid.*

3 *Ibid.*

4 *Title IX at 25: Report Card on Gender Equity* (Washington, D.C.: National Coalition for Women and Girls in Education, 1997), 2.

5 U.S. Department of Education, National Center for Education Statistics, *Fall Enrollment in Post Secondary Education, 1997* (Washington, D.C., 1999).

6 U.S. Department of Education, *Title IX: 25 Years of Progress* (Washington, D.C., 1997).

7 *Ibid.*

8 *Ibid.*

9 *Profile of 1998 SAT Test Takers* (New York: College Board, 1998).

10 U.S. Department of Education, *National Assessment of Vocational Education* (Washington, D.C., 1992).

11 *Hostile Hallways: The AAUW Survey on Sexual Harassment in America's Schools* (Washington, D.C.: American Association of University Women Educational Foundation, 1993); W. A. Brown and J. Maestro-Scherer, Assessing Sexual Harassment and Public Safety: A Survey of Cornell Women (Ithaca, N.Y.: Cornell University Office of Equal Opportunity, 1986).

12 U.S. Department of Education, *Digest of Education Statistics, 1998* (Washington, D.C., 1998).

13 Iram Valentin, "Title IX: A Brief History," *Women's Educational Equity Act Digest* (1997).

14 *Ibid.*

15 *Ibid.*

16 Verna L. Williams, Leslie T. Annexstein, and Neena Chaudhary, "The Continuing Challenge: Gender Equity in Education and the Clinton Administration," in *The Test of Our Progress: The Clinton Record on Civil Rights* (Washington, D.C.: Citizens' Commission on Civil Rights, 1999).

17 U.S. Department of Education, Office for Civil Rights, *Annual Report to Congress: Fiscal Year 1994* (Washington, D.C., 1994).

18 *Grove City College v. Bell,* 465 U.S. 555 (1984).

19 *Franklin v. Gwinnett County Public Schools,* 503 U.S. 60 (1992).

20 *Gebser v. Lago Vista Independent School District,* 524 U.S. 274 (1998).

21 *Franklin v. Gwinnett County Public Schools,* 503 U.S. 60 (1992).

22 *Gebser v. Lago Vista Independent School District,* 524 U.S. 274 (1998).

23 *Burlington Industries, Inc. v. Ellerth,* 524 U.S. 775 (1998) and *Faragher v. City Of Boca Raton,* 524 U.S. 742 (1998).

24 *Davis v. Monroe County Board of Education,* 119 S. Ct. 1661 (1999).

25 U.S. Department of Education, Office for Civil Rights, *Annual Report to Congress: Fiscal Year 1998* (Washington, D.C., 1998).

26 *Summary of the Regulations for Title IX.*

27 Data from the Office for Civil Rights (1993-1997).

28 U.S. Department of Education, Office for Civil Rights, *Case Resolution Manual* (Washington, D.C., 1998).

29 *Ibid.*

30 *Ibid.*

31 OCR, *Annual Report to Congress: 1998.*

Chapter One: Who's Complaining?

1 U.S. Department of Education, Office for Civil Rights, *Annual Reports to Congress: Fiscal Years 1994-1998* (Washington, D.C.).

2 *Ibid.*

3 Data from the Office for Civil Rights (1993-1997).

4 *Summary of the Regulations for Title IX.*

5 OCR, *Annual Report to Congress, 1998.*

6 Based on our sample.

7 Based on our sample.

Chapter 2: Trends and Issues in Title IX Complaints

1 *Hostile Hallways; In Our Own Backyard: Sexual Harassment In Connecticut's Public High Schools* (Hartford: Permanent Commission on the Status of Women, 1995); M. Trigg and K. Wittenstrom, "That's the Way the World Really Goes: Sexual Harassment and New Jersey Teenagers," *Initiatives* 57 (1996): 2, 55-65.

2 *Hostile Hallways.*

3 *Hostile Hallways; In Our Own Backyard:* Trigg and Wittenstrom, "That's The Way The World Really Goes," 55-65.

4 *Hostile Hallways;* Brown, "Assessing Sexual Harassment and Public Safety"; B. A. Gutek, *Sex and the Workplace* (San Francisco: Jossey-Bass, 1985).

5 *Hostile Hallways; In Our Own Backyard;* Trigg and Wittenstrom, "That's The Way The World Really Goes," 55-65.

6 N. D. Stein, N. Marshall, and L. Tropp, *Secrets in Public: Sexual Harassment in Our Schools* (Wellesley, Mass.: Wellesley College Center for Research on Women, 1993).

7 *Hostile Hallways.*

8 *Ibid.*

9 *Federal sex discrimination laws do not protect against discrimination on the basis of sexual orientation, although some state and local statutes do.* See Bernice Sandler and Robert Shoop, eds., *Sexual Harassment on Campus: A Guide for Administrators, Faculty, and Students* (Washington, D.C.: National Association for Women in Education, 1997).

10 U.S. Department of Education, Office for Civil Rights, *Sexual Harassment Guidance: Harassment of Students by School Employees, Other Students, or Third Parties* (Washington, D.C., 1997).

11 *Ibid.*

12 *Ibid.*

13 S. J. Smith, "Title IX and Sexual Harassment," *Women's Educational Equity Act Digest* (1998).

14 OCR, *Sexual Harassment Guidance.*

15 Stein, Marshall, and Tropp, *Secrets in Public.*

16 *Profile of 1998 SAT Test Takers.*

17 H. Stumpf and J. C. Stanley, "Gender-Related Differences on the College Board's Advanced Placement and Achievement Tests, 1982-1992," *Journal of Educational Psychology* 88 (1996): 2, 353-364.

18 M. J. Clark and J. Grandy, *Sex Differences in the Academic Performance of Scholastic Aptitude Test Takers* (New York: College Board Publications, 1984); R. Elliot and A. C. Strenta, "Effects of

Improving the Reliability of the GPA on Prediction Generally and on Comparative Predictions for Gender and Race Particularly," *Journal of Educational Measurement* 25 (1988): 4, 333-47; D. K. Leonard and J. Jiang, "Gender Bias in College Predictions of the SAT," (paper presented to the annual conference of the American Educational Research Association, San Francisco, 1995); L. Stricker, D. Rock, and N. Burton, *Sex Differences in SAT Predictions of College Grades* (New York: College Entrance Examination Board, 1991); H. Wainer and L. S. Steinberg, "Sex Differences in Performance on the Mathematics Section of the Scholastic Aptitude Test: A Bi-Directional Validity Study," *Harvard Educational Review* 62 (1991): 3, 323-336; W. W. Willingham, C. Lewis, R. Morgan, and L. Ramist, *Predicting College Grades: An Analysis of Institutional Trends Over Two Decades* (Princeton: Educational Testing Service, 1990).

19 Myra Sadker and David Sadker, *Failing at Fairness: How Our Schools Cheat Girls* (New York: Touchstone, 1994).

20 Clark and Grandy, *Sex Differences in the Academic Performance*; Elliot and Strenta, "Effects of Improving the Reliability of the GPA"; Leonard and Jiang, "Gender Bias"; Stricker, Rock, and Burton, *Sex Differences in SAT Predictions*; Wainer and Steinberg, "Sex Differences in Performance"; Willingham, et al., *Predicting College Grades*.

21 See National Women's Law Center's Petition in Support of Certiorari filed in *Kirwan v. Podberesky*, 94-1620, 94-1621 (1995).

22 Clark and Grandy, *Sex Differences in the Academic Performance*; Elliot and Strenta, "Effects of Improving the Reliability of the GPA"; Leonard and Jiang, "Gender Bias"; Stricker, Rock, and Burton, *Sex Differences in SAT Predictions*; Wainer and Steinberg, "Sex Differences in Performance"; Willingham, et al., *Predicting College Grades*.

23 "PSAT Revisions Further Narrow Gender Gap," *FairTest Examiner* (Summer 1999).

24 "Gender Bias Victory Wins Millions for Females But National Merit Test Remains Biased," *FairTest Examiner* (Spring 1999).

25 Clark and Grandy, *Sex Differences in the Academic Performance*; Elliot and Strenta, "Effects of Improving the Reliability of the GPA"; Leonard and Jiang, "Gender Bias"; Stricker, Rock, and Burton, *Sex Differences in SAT Predictions*; Wainer and Steinberg, "Sex Differences in Performance"; Willingham, et al., *Predicting College Grades*.

26 Sadker and Sadker, *Failing at Fairness*.

27 *Ibid.*

28 *Ibid.*

29 U.S. Department of Education, Office for Civil Rights, *1994 Elementary and Secondary School Civil Rights Compliance Report* (Washington, D.C., 1994).

30 *Ibid.*

31 Sadker and Sadker, *Failing at Fairness*.

32 U.S. Department of Education, National Center for Education Statistics, *Women in Mathematics and Science* (Washington, D.C., 1997).

33 *Profile of 1998 SAT Test Takers.*

34 U.S. Department of Education, *Digest of Education Statistics.*

35 *Women, Minorities, and Persons With Disabilities in Science and Engineering: 1996* (Arlington, VA: National Science Foundation, 1996).

36 P. Rayman and B. Brett, "Women Science Majors," *Journal of Higher Education* 66 (1995): 4, 388-414; E. Seymour and N. M. Hewitt, *Talking About Leaving: Why Undergraduates Leave the Sciences* (Boulder: Westview Press, 1997).

37 *Gender Gaps: Where Schools Still Fail Our Children* (Washington, D.C.: American Association of University Women Educational Foundation, 1999).

38 U.S. Department of Education, National Center for Education Statistics, *National Assessment of Vocational Education* (Washington, D.C., 1992).

39 *Title IX at 25: Report Card on Gender Equity:* 17.

40 U.S. Department of Education, *Digest of Education Statistics*.

41 *Ibid.*

42 *Ibid.*

43 *Ibid.*

44 Benjamin Ernst, "Disparities in the Salaries and Appointments of Academic Women and Men: An Update of a 1988 Report of Committee W on the Status of Women in the Academic Profession," *Academe: Bulletin of the American Association of University Professors*, January-February 1999.

45 "Tips to Help Research Universities Support Women Faculty," *Women in Higher Education* 8, no. 1 (January 1999): 1.

46 Ernst, "Disparities in the Salaries."

47 U.S. Department of Education, *Title IX at 25*.

48 Ernst, "Disparities in the Salaries."

49 Committee on Women Faculty, *A Study on the Status of Women Faculty in the Sciences at MIT* (Cambridge: Massachusetts Institute of Technology, 1999).

50 *North Haven v. Bell*, 456 U.S. 512 (1982).

Chapter Three: OCR Investigation of Title IX Complaints

1 OCR, *Case Resolution Manual*.

2 Generally, the statute of limitations for Title IX is the same as the most similar cause of action under state law. Most states look to personal injury law to determine a statute of limitations for Title IX cases (e.g. *Bougher v. University of Pennsylvania*, 882 F2d 74, 77 (3rd Cir 1989)).

3 OCR, *Annual Report to Congress: 1998*.

4 OCR, *Case Resolution Manual*.

5 *Ibid.*

6 *Ibid.*

7 *Ibid.*

8 Schools and universities may be responding in part to confidentiality concerns by not maintaining these records, but this information can be collected and disseminated without identifying the parties involved.

Chapter Four: Resolution and Monitoring of Complaints

1 OCR, *Case Resolution Manual*.

2 *The Women's Sports Foundation Report on Title IX, Athletics, and the Office for Civil Rights* (Washington, D.C.: Women's Sports Foundation, 1997).

Chapter Five: Action Agenda for Title IX

1 OCR, *Annual Report to Congress: 1998*.

2 U.S. Department of Education, *Office for Civil Rights, Annual Report to Congress: Fiscal Year 1993* (Washington, D.C., 1993).

3 N. P. Stromquist, "Sex-Equity Legislation in Education: The State as Promoter of Women's Rights," *Review of Educational Research* 63 (1993): 4, 379-407.

4 Women's Educational Equity Act Resource Center, 1999. A list of state equity contacts appears on the WEEA website at http://www.edc.org/womensequity/resource/title 9/state.htm

5 Williams, Annexstein, and Chaudhary, "The Continuing Challenge."

6 Stein, Marshall, and Tropp, *Secrets in Public*.

AAUW Legal Advocacy Fund
Board of Directors

Sylvia Newman, President

Undine Stinnette, Vice President

Marilyn S. Arp, Co-Finance Vice President

Michele Wetherald, Secretary

Sylvia McDowell

Mary Beth O'Quinn

Ex Officio: Sandy Bernard, AAUW President

The AAUW Legal Advocacy Fund provides funding and a support system for women seeking judicial redress for sex discrimination.

In principle and practice, the AAUW Legal Advocacy Fund values and seeks the support of a diverse AAUW membership. There shall be no barriers to full participation in this organization on the basis of gender, race, creed, age, sexual orientation, national origin, or disability.

AAUW LEGAL ADVOCACY FUND

American Association of University Women Legal Advocacy Fund
1111 Sixteenth St. N.W.
Washington, DC 20036
202/785-7750
Fax: 202/785-8754
TDD: 202/785-7777
laf@aauw.org
www.aauw.org

AAUW Equity Library

A License for Bias: Sex Discrimination, Schools, and Title IX
Examines uneven efforts to implement the 1972 civil rights law that protects some 70 million students and employees from sex discrimination in schools and universities. The analysis of non-sports-related complaints filed between 1993 and 1997 pinpoints problems that hamper enforcement and includes recommendations for Congress, the Office for Civil Rights, and educational institutions. Published by the AAUW Legal Advocacy Fund.
60 pages/Winter 2000.
$11.95 members/$12.95 nonmembers.

¡Sí, Se Puede!/Yes, We Can: Latinas in School
by Angela Ginorio and Michelle Huston
Comprehensive look at the status of Latina girls in the U.S. public education system. Report explores conflicts between institutional expectations and the realities of student lives, and discusses the social, cultural, and community factors that affect Hispanic education. Published in English and Spanish.
80 pages/Winter 2000.
$11.95 members/$12.95 nonmembers

Community Coalitions Manual With Lessons Learned From the Girls Can! Project
A comprehensive guide for establishing and sustaining effective coalition-based programs. Covers volunteer recruitment, project planning, evaluation, fundraising, and public relations, with contact information for more than 200 organizations, and lessons learned from the Girls Can! Community Coalitions Projects, a nationwide gender equity program.
166 pages/Winter 2000.
$14.95 AAUW members/$16.95 nonmembers.

Tech-Savvy: Educating Girls in the New Computer Age
Explores girls' and teachers' perspectives of today's computer culture and technology use at school, home, and work. Gives recommendations for broadening access to computers for girls and others who don't fit the "male hacker/computer geek" stereotype.
100 pages/2000.
$11.95 members/$12.95 nonmembers.

Voices of a Generation: Teenage Girls on Sex, School, and Self
Compares the comments of roughly 2,100 girls nationwide on peer pressure, sexuality, the media, and school. The girls were 1997 and 1998 participants in AAUW teen forums called Sister-to-Sister Summits. The report explores differences in girls' responses by race, ethnicity, and age and offers the girls' action proposals to solve common problems.
95 pages/1999.
$13.95 members/$14.95 nonmembers.

Gaining a Foothold: Women's Transitions Through Work and College
Examines how and why women make changes in their lives through education. The report profiles three groups—women going from high school to college, from high school to work, and from work to education—using both quantitative and qualitative methods. Findings include an analysis of women's educational decisions, aspirations, and barriers.
100 pages/1999.
$11.95 members/$12.95 nonmembers.

Higher Education in Transition: The Politics and Practices of Equity Symposium Proceedings
A compilation of papers presented at AAUW's June 1999 higher education symposium in Washington, D.C. Topics addressed include campus climate and multiculturalism, higher education faculty and success, higher education student retention and success, and the effect of equity issues on higher education curricula and classrooms.
390 pages/1999.
$19.95 members/$21.95 nonmembers.

Gender Gaps: Where Schools Still Fail Our Children

Measures schools' mixed progress toward gender equity and excellence since the 1992 publication of *How Schools Shortchange Girls*. Report compares student course enrollments, tests, grades, risks, and resiliency by race and class as well as gender. It finds some gains in girls' achievement, some areas where boys—not girls—lag, and some areas, like technology, where needs have not yet been addressed.
150 pages/1998.
$12.95 members/$13.95 nonmembers.

Separated By Sex: A Critical Look at Single-Sex Education for Girls

The foremost educational scholars on single-sex education in grades K-12 compare findings on whether girls learn better apart from boys. The report, including a literature review and a summary of a forum convened by the AAUW Educational Foundation, challenges the popular idea that single-sex education is better for girls than coeducation.
99 pages/1998.
$11.95 AAUW members/$12.95 nonmembers.

Gender and Race on the Campus and in the School: Beyond Affirmative Action Symposium Proceedings

A compilation of papers presented at AAUW's June 1997 college/university symposium in Anaheim. Symposium topics include K-12 curricula and student achievement, positive gender and race awareness in elementary and secondary school, campus climate and multiculturalism, higher education student retention and success, and the nexus of race and gender in higher education curricula and classrooms.
428 pages/1997.
$19.95 AAUW members/$21.95 nonmembers.

Girls in the Middle: Working to Succeed in School

Engaging study of middle school girls and the strategies they use to meet the challenges of adolescence. Report links girls' success to school reforms like team teaching and cooperative learning, especially where these are used to address gender issues.
128 pages/1996.
$12.95 AAUW members /$14.95 nonmembers.

Gender Gaps Executive Summary

Overview of *Gender Gaps* report with selected findings, tables, bibliography, and recommendations for educators and policy-makers.
24 pages/1998.
$6.95 members/$7.95 nonmembers.

How Schools Shortchange Girls: The AAUW Report

Marlowe paperback edition. A startling examination of how girls are disadvantaged in America's schools, grades K-12. Includes recommendations for educators and policy-makers as well as concrete strategies for change.
240 pages/1995.
$11.95 AAUW members/$12.95 nonmembers.

Hostile Hallways: The AAUW Survey on Sexual Harassment in America's Schools

The first national study of sexual harassment in school, based on the experiences of 1,632 students in grades 8 through 11. Gender and ethnic/racial (African American, Hispanic, and white) data breakdowns included. Commissioned by the AAUW Educational Foundation and conducted by Louis Harris and Associates.
28 pages/1993.
$8.95 AAUW members/$11.95 nonmembers.

SchoolGirls: Young Women, Self-Esteem, and the Confidence Gap

Doubleday, 1994. Riveting book by journalist Peggy Orenstein in association with AAUW shows how girls in two racially and economically diverse California communities suffer the painful plunge in self-esteem documented in *Shortchanging Girls, Shortchanging America*.
384 pages/1994.
$11.95 AAUW members/$12.95 nonmembers.

Shortchanging Girls, Shortchanging America Executive Summary

Summary of the 1991 poll that assesses self-esteem, educational experiences, and career aspirations of girls and boys ages 9-15. Revised edition reviews poll's impact, offers action strategies, and highlights survey results with charts and graphs.
20 pages/1994.
$8.95 AAUW members/$11.95 nonmembers.

Order Form

Name_____ AAUW membership # (if applicable) _____

Street _____

City/State/ZIP _____

Daytime phone (_____)_____ E-mail_____

Item	Price Member/Nonmember	Quantity	Total
A License for Bias	$11.95/$12.95	_____	_____
¡Sí, Se Puede!/Yes, We Can	$11.95/$12.95	_____	_____
Community Coalitions Manual	$14.95/$16.95	_____	_____
Tech-Savvy	$11.95/$12.95	_____	_____
Voices of a Generation	$13.95/$14.95	_____	_____
Gaining a Foothold	$11.95/$12.95	_____	_____
Higher Education in Transition	$19.95/$21.95	_____	_____
Gender Gaps	$12.95/$13.95	_____	_____
Separated By Sex	$11.95/$12.95	_____	_____
Gender and Race on the Campus and in the School	$19.95/$21.95	_____	_____
Girls in the Middle	$12.95/$14.95	_____	_____
Gender Gaps Executive Summary	$6.95/$7.95	_____	_____
How Schools Shortchange Girls	$11.95/$12.95	_____	_____
Hostile Hallways	$8.95/$11.95	_____	_____
SchoolGirls	$11.95/$12.95	_____	_____
Shortchanging Girls Executive Summary	$8.95/$11.95	_____	_____

Subtotal ($25 minimum): _____

Sales Tax: _____

Shipping/Handling (see chart below): _____

Total Order: _____

For bulk pricing on orders of 10 or more, call 800/225-9998 ext. 530.

For rush orders, call 800/225-9998 ext. 530. A $5 fee plus actual shipping charges will apply.

Shipments to foreign countries are sent surface rate and postage is charged at cost plus a $15 handling charge.

All applicable duties and taxes are paid by customer.

AAUW Federal Identification Number: 53-0025390.

❑ Check/Money Order (Please make payable in U.S. currency to Newton Manufacturing Co. Do not send cash.)

❑ MasterCard/Visa   Card #___ ___ ___ ___ - ___ ___ ___ ___ - ___ ___ ___ ___ - ___ ___ ___ ___ Expiration_____

Name on card _____

Cardholder signature _____

SATISFACTION GUARANTEED: If you are not completely satisfied with your purchase, please return it within 90 days for exchange, credit, or refund. Videos are returnable only if defective, and for replacement only.

FOR MAIL ORDERS, SEND THIS FORM TO:
AAUW Sales Office
Newton Manufacturing Co.
P.O. Box 927
Newton, IA 50208-0927

FOR TELEPHONE ORDERS, CALL:
800/225-9998 ext. 530
800/500-5118 fax

TO ORDER ONLINE:
www.aauw.org